ZIMBABWE

AFRICA IS RICH
AFRICANS ARE POOR

By

Richard Boidin

Translated by
Marie Kuhn-Osius

Tambar

ISBN 978-1-910133-26-2

Tambar Arts Ltd: Reg. No. 03937329

Publication date: April 2024

www.tambar.co.uk

e-mail: contact@tambar.co.uk

*For Tendaï,
who opened so many doors for me*

CONTENTS

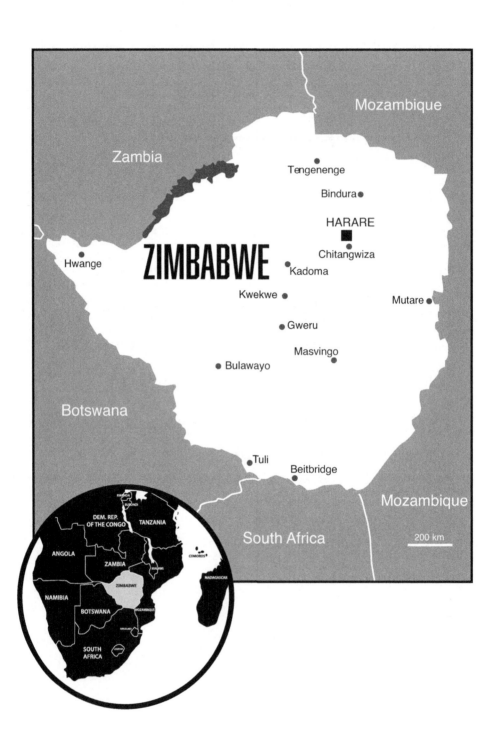

PROLOGUE

'Woe is me! I am *a nuance.*'
Friedrich Nietzsche, *Ecce homo*
(published in English as: *Ecce Homo*)

Writing about Zimbabwe and Africa amounts to asking for trouble, especially for me as a white person who used to officially represent France, whose colonial past has left indelible traces wherever we look.

I can already hear people saying, 'Here goes yet another white person who wants to explain Africa to Africans!' and that isn't wrong. Surely I had better just stay silent - and perhaps simply beat my chest in repentance.

But I can't leave it at that.

In truth, I have a moral obligation to tell my story because of the sheer amount of suffering that the people of Zimbabwe have been through.

As a powerless observer of a daily life which, at times, was enough to drive anyone to hopelessness, I had to reconsider most of my positions. Zimbabwe compelled me toward humility each and every day.

I had thought that I had a good grasp and a solid perspective and was convinced that my thirty years on various missions in Africa had given me a certain degree of expertise.

This was not the case.

True reality, of which I had only had a glimpse on my previous short trips, forced itself on me in its harshest light once I had to live through it on a daily basis.

In Zimbabwe I had to take into account a certain number of grave and complicated issues: an opaque political system, a people who had been deprived of their own history, pernicious international economic aid, demographic growth, and endemic corruption.

My understanding of the world I had been thrust into could easily have remained incomplete had it not been for something unexpected that happened.

A chance encounter with a man from Zimbabwe saved me a lot of time. He called into question the few basic propositions that I had thought to be the most widely accepted: the existence of the African Union, the pedestal of black identity, the relationship with the West and the true impact of slavery and colonisation.

This man was a member of the Shona – the main ethnic group in Zimbabwe. He is a veteran of the war of liberation, an alert man in his seventies with a physique as wizened as the branches of an acacia tree.

I'll call him Tendaï (it is best to conceal his true identity). He was to be a legitimate and intelligent contrarian, equally lively and ruthless in his thinking.

I first met Tendaï in Tengenenge*. He was sitting on a slab of rock next to a woman sculptor who was working on a piece of serpentine under the admiring gaze of three tourists. As I came closer, I overheard the enthusiastic praises of these three tourists, who expressed their admiration for such age-old and authentic African art. Tendaï stood up and taunted them.

'African art? What do you mean African art? This is a Shona sculpture!'

It is well known that tourists are easily scared. Without much ado, the three of them beat a quick retreat. I couldn't help giving Tendaï a smile. In Zimbabwe, where courtesy is a golden rule, a smile is the key that opens any door.

We had a cheery, relaxed conversation about this and that until I mentioned my profession.

Tendaï abruptly ended our chat with a curt question. 'Excuse me, what would you like to buy here?'

---

*The village of Tengenenge is located in northeastern Zimbabwe. It was founded in the late 1960s by a remarkable white man named Tom Blomefield and was a village of sculptors that for decades brought together the greatest artists who worked on so-called soft stones, including serpentine. Mr Blomefield was supported in his endeavor by the director of the National Gallery of the time, a Scotsman named Frank McEwen. McEwen was to lose his position – this was before independence – for having given great visibility to the sculpture of these lowly black farmers, who had, with Mr Blomefield's help, been transformed into world-renowned artists who garnered praise from the Surrealists. This village still stands today, but it is only a shadow of its former self. It consists of some dilapidated dwellings, rudimentary art studios and an outdoor exhibition area for a few sculptors. Why has this village been deliberately neglected by the authorities? I have sometimes wondered if it was seen as a threat to the dogmas of the liberation ideology of the party in power that the international recognition of these black sculptors in the art world was owed to two white men in the colonial era of Rhodesia.

Armed with a statuette, for which I must have paid twice the normal price, I went on my way and left behind my business card with my work mobile number on it.

One month later, to my great surprise, I got a call from Tendaï. I thought to myself, 'it must be another visa request'. But, no - he just wanted to get to know me over lunch.

We kept meeting on and off for nearly three years. Sometimes he would bring a relative along.

Those relatives were often young and never said a thing.

Each time, Tendaï would call me from a different telephone number. He claimed not to have a mobile. I doubted this, but that is the way it was.

Our encounters were erratic. Upon his request, we would meet in some modest snack-bar in various shopping arcades of his choosing. In Tendaï's mind, engaging in a relationship with an official representative of the West - even a casual one - seemed to require utmost prudence.

Many times I tried to explain to him that the status of an ambassador was not as important as he imagined. To no avail. I could have told him that, ambassador or not, I would become an ordinary citizen once I was back in France. I refrained from doing so, however, since I had been discouraged by a previous explanation that he had challenged. He considered me to be more important than I was. That must have suited him.

That's how our discussions took shape. Tendaï wanted to explain Zimbabwe and Africa to me.

From his point of view, white people don't understand any of it. As for me, I critically challenged his ideas and emotions to their very limits.

Our dialogue was unsparing. Usually we 'fenced' with capped foils and at times there was a certain bad faith. Given the wide range of topics we addressed, I sometimes felt as though Bouvard and Pécuchet, the famous characters from Gustave Flaubert's novel, had been transported to Harare to discuss the state of Africa.

A Shona statue

To best reflect how my experience developed, each chapter starts off with my experience in the field. Thanks to Tendaï's elevated point of view, I was able to expand my horizons and broach a wide range of topics concerning Africa.

I consider giving my testimony to be a matter of necessity because the people of Zimbabwe cannot and must not be abandoned. But I have not forgotten something essential. I am and always will be a European - with the inescapable consequence that my understanding is limited.

PROLOGUE

CHAPTER I

MACBETH, THE AFRICAN

*'Power tends to corrupt, and
absolute power corrupts absolutely.'*
Lord Acton

Almost five centuries of slavery and colonisation have left the people of Africa little respite. These terrible hardships still dominate the mental landscape of numerous people, as is the case in Zimbabwe.

Recognising these tragedies, however, does not dispense us from taking note that, since gaining independence, the peoples' hopes for emancipation are still far from being fulfilled. This is because most of the current regimes have reached a point of exhaustion, after shamelessly playing the colonial debt card to mask their failures, greed and carelessness.

The best of intentions may motivate a war for independence. However, after that battle is won, they can be devoured in a classical manner, by the eternal mechanics of power: getting power - whether legitimately or not - then giving oneself the means to exercise it, and finally doing all it takes to maintain it.

Then the political, commercial and military elites focus on maintaining their own privilege, disregarding the populations they serve.

This is the situation I noticed when I arrived in Zimbabwe in November 2016.

There were two worlds which cohabited without seeking to live together: the world of the leaders, a tight-knit and suspicious circle, living a lavish lifestyle and sequestered in certain residential areas; and the world of most people, who were focused on surviving and were either crowded into the outskirts of the cities or isolated in the remote countryside.

Between these two worlds, there was a small urban middle class, a sort of petty bourgeoisie, struggling to maintain its position.

When remembering Zimbabwe, most visitors think of the beautiful scenery - at least the famous Victoria Falls - or the incredible presence of wild plants and animals in their natural state. That is undeniable.

As for me, I would highlight the courtesy and kindness of the people. I learned true life lessons through my daily contact with people who exhibited no discernible trace of aggressiveness. It would be tempting to think that they are people who have thrown in the towel.

That is far from the truth. Since the early 2000s, they have regularly tried to protest, demanding more decent living conditions, and every time they were ruthlessly suppressed - often with real bullets. It was a choice between death or exile, a large number chose the second solution.

To justify the rapid pauperisation of the country, the regime systematically blamed sanctions by the West, starting with those by the United States. This is obviously false.

We must recall that the sanctions by the West, whose content I will address later, were largely motivated by the great violence surrounding the general elections of 2008. The party in power, sensing a loss of its position, went into such a rage that the democratic opposition, although it had won, preferred to withdraw to avoid a blood bath.

One man was at the heart of this implacable system of domination: Robert Mugabe. From independence in 1980 until his retirement in 2017, he ruled the country with an iron fist, supported by his party, the Zanu-PF (Zimbabwe African National Union-Patriotic Front).

In February 2017, I knew I would have to face this man, aged and very ill, but just as charismatic and feared as ever. My meeting with him in his presidential palace - a vast building built in a very British colonial style - would not be an ordinary one.

After waiting for nearly five hours in an overheated room together with four other ambassadors who were also there to present their credentials, I lost my patience and demanded some water and nourishment. There followed a lengthy negotiation with the protocol representatives, interrupted by the arrival of three military vehicles with heavily armed soldiers belonging to the presidential guard, who positioned themselves near us. So there was no point in insisting.

The instructions were to wait, and these were strictly enforced. President Robert Mugabe would arrive at long last. He would receive us one by one.

When it was my turn - two hours later - I was dehydrated and hungry. But it didn't matter. The ritual of presenting credentials would soon be over.

The presentation took place in a sort of unreal flutter because there was nothing straight-forward about finding oneself in front of the most implacable African head of state, 'a certified master of violence', as Robert Mugabe liked to style himself.

The exchange began on a cold note because he accused the West, including the French, of imposing illegitimate sanctions on his country.

The most astonishing thing was the rate of his speech. He would start a sentence and then interrupt himself in the middle of it, overcome by a sharp pain, which disabled his limbs. He struggled to control the painful spasms that shot through his body. Some ten seconds later - once his convulsions were more or less under control - he would pick up his statement where he had left off, precisely resuming the thread of his reasoning, expressing himself in a most elaborate English.

An impressive exercise of staunch will.

He followed up with his obsession: the English.

In a heavy atmosphere, about twenty ministers of Zimbabwe were sitting right across from us. Their armchairs were positioned in a horseshoe shape as they listened with bowed heads to the jerky and repetitive words of their dreaded leader. It was hard for me to believe that they were still under the sway of this 93-year-old man who was to die two years later.

Tired of hearing the long litany of reproaches of all types against the English prime ministers who came after Margaret Thatcher, I had the temerity, in a moment of folly, to interrupt the great leader. I realised the enormity of the crime of lèse-majesté when I perceived the grief-stricken looks which the Zimbabwean hierarchs cast at me. Robert Mugabe looked at me with such intensity that I cursed my impatience that so often gets the better of me.

I had the nerve to say, 'If you would like, Your Excellency, I have at your disposal the list of endless atrocities that the English did to us French people.'

Robert Mugabe's amused smile in response to this spontaneous interjection lessened the tension of the assembly immediately. The second part of the interview proceeded in a much more relaxed atmosphere.

The President of Zimbabwe loved good retorts and proceeded to ask me the following question.

'Do you know why the English are so inept?' he murmured.

Despite the upheavals of his ill body, he managed to continue.

'Because you can't expect anything intelligent from a nation that worships hot water!'

He continued to twist around on his chair. His eyes lit up in mockery. The assembly burst out into full-throated laughter, too loud to be sincere. I joined in the laughter, as a matter of courtesy.

I avoided paying attention to the cup of tea perched between us on a side table that was still emitting steam and which a server kept refilling as the old man drank it up with great pleasure.

At this very moment, something unexpected happened. Still subject to uncontrolled contortions, as if struggling against his own body, he stretched out his arm in my direction and took my hand. It was like being touched by the limp tentacle of a dead octopus. I did not dare withdraw my hand, I still had to make a good impression.

And so during the remaining twenty minutes of the interview, we exchanged the usual niceties, hand in hand - he in the grip of the total war that was ravaging his body, and I trying not to look into his yellowed eyes, convinced that I was facing a giant python that would strangle me if I dared to meet his gaze.

I had one last fright during this formal encounter when, still holding my hand, he again interrupted his speech, but this time without moving a single muscle in his body for about a minute. 'He's dead,' I thought, 'and I'm holding his hand!'

The fear of being associated with his death - with all of its fateful consequences - incapacitated me. I stared at one of the windows, completely unable to move, in the hope of being swallowed by my armchair.

But no, he woke up again and continued as if nothing had happened, and without losing beat, he resumed his analysis of his country's links with France.

To finish the ceremony, we headed to the garden of the presidential palace for the official photograph. It's impossible for me to describe the sense of culpability that overtook me as I had to stand next to him and pose for a sort of family photo with this ruthless dictator. Of course, it was not I personally posing in this manner, but the political entity that I was representing. Yet still, it was surely I who was standing next to Robert Mugabe for the photo to be taken.

It left a bitter taste in my mouth when I received a compliment from one of the regime's strong men. As I was leaving the presidential palace after the ceremony, he called out to me in a jovial tone, 'Great first contact! You will do great things with us.'

Less than a year later, this same person was to be actively involved in sidelining Mugabe.

I told the story of the presentation of my credentials to Tendaï more than once, but he never got enough of it. Both before and after Robert Mugabe was removed from power in November 2017, he asked me to return to this event, as if, through me, he could still feel the presence of Robert Mugabe, whom he called by his nickname 'Bob'.

Tendaï could afford to use the nickname because he was a member of the party in power, the Zanu-PF - commonly called the Zanu. What's more, he was an original veteran, one of the fearsome and dreaded 'war vets'. Thus, Bob was one of his old comrades.

Tall and lean, Tendaï always walked with measured steps and was modestly dressed. His emaciated face was dominated by his lively expression. Our meetings had an air of secrecy to them. In fact, an unknowing onlooker could have thought that I was an officer dealing with a local dissident. Tendaï took care to nurture this comedy, perhaps seeking to relive the years of his youth when he roamed the bush, hunted by white militias and the secret service of Rhodesia.

I played along out of respect for this man in his seventies who, unlike practically all his comrades, had not taken advantage of his status to get rich scrupulously.

As often as I explained to him that I had access to the top circles of the Zanu without running into any problems, he would reply that I was naive.

So I would meet up with him under the conditions set by his minor paranoia.

And so we found ourselves to be in the habit of meeting over mediocre meals at one of those supermarket snack counters. He would eat at a slow pace, whilst the occasional young 'guest' he brought along would wolf down the food. As for me, my main nourishment was the conversation, as I did not much fancy the overly salted food in these snack-bars. No matter how insistently I offered to invite Tendaï to a fancier restaurant, he would not budge. He also categorically rejected my invitations to the French Residence.

Did he perhaps just want to meet me in public, in a crowd? Did he perhaps refuse to profit from the situation by getting himself invited to a real restaurant? Did he perhaps want to keep a distance between himself and me? All of these reasons are certainly plausible. In any case, we both greatly enjoyed watching his young guests devour their meals ravenously.

I would have wanted to do more for Tendaï and the people close to him. But I had to accept his limits there, too. He just wanted us to meet to exchange ideas but without intruding into each others' lives.

In the month of January 2019 over a year had passed since Robert Mugabe had been divested of his powers and retired to his luxurious mansion, the Blue Roof, in the upscale district of Borrowdale, in northeastern Harare.

The city had just experienced violent police repression against the population in its poorest quarters. Spurred by destitution, these riots gave rise to many scenes of looting of shops and petrol stations.

'Tell me the story of your meeting with Comrade Bob again.'

I refused outright to speak of Robert Mugabe because, even if he was no longer in power, it was he who in the years since independence had set up this system of brutal domination which his colleagues in the Zanu were eagerly reinforcing after his departure.

To my great surprise, I was for the first time met with vehement protestations in which Tendaï explained something to me. Bob was an unacceptable dictator or worse for us Westerners and an incarnation of the devil for the white people of southern Africa, but, in stark contrast, he was a true idol for the people of Zimbabwe and for all the black people of Africa.

The proof for this, he said, was that he was always welcomed like a rockstar throughout Africa. And that wasn't wrong. Tendaï's vehemence was not feigned, and I still remember one of his scathing remarks: 'And do you know why we have such admiration for him? It's because he's the only African leader who dared to kick all the white people out of his country! Look at South Africa today. They're biting their fingers with regret that they didn't do it. They will get to it. And so will the other African countries.'

Given his agitation, I didn't want to contradict him or play the role of a white person who was offended by this overtly racist affirmation. Rather, I wondered what could have triggered my interlocutor to be so blinkered, as he generally was more measured in his analysis. I understood that Tendaï would not tolerate having the image of his hero denigrated.

Many times he returned to the topic of the war of liberation and the role Bob and his comrades played in it, emphasising that we Westerners would not pay enough attention to the traumatic legacy of colonisation and to the immense sacrifices that were willingly incurred during the struggles for independence.

Tendaï regained his composure and tried to justify his point of view.

He brought up the period after independence, in the 1980s, when Bob, the pragmatic unifier, tried, according to him, to convince white people to share the economic power, of which they were in complete control.

About 6,000 white farmers owned vast commercial farms on the best land and ran the economy of a prosperous country that exported many agricultural goods of the highest quality. Wasn't it known as the bread basket of southern Africa?

But, lo and behold, the white farmers had different ideas and Bob soon came to see them as a dangerous adversary that threatened his control. Since then, the question of land redistribution took on a dimension of internal politics that was vital for the Zanu; they felt pressure from the white apartheid regime in South Africa, which served as a rear base for the white people of Zimbabwe.

The African National Congress's (ANC) rise to power in Pretoria in the 1990s changed the situation. The white farmers in Zimbabwe were now alone in their opposition to the authorities in Harare.

In the early 2000s, Bob was still frustrated by the obstruction from the white farmers - and, in addition, worried about the increasing power of an opposition party (the Movement for Democratic Change, MDC, founded by Morgan Tsvangirai, a union activist from Zimbabwe who died in 2018). He decided to expel the farmers with military force, leading to the mass exodus of 200,000 people.

'For twenty years - that's twenty years - he waited for the white people to be willing to share!... They did not want to. And so he kicked them out.'

Tendaï repeated his assertion twice in a grave tone - as if it did not warrant any response.

And so it would have been pointless for me to remind him that the first expropriations had started in the 1990s, that the funds provided by the British during those years and meant to finance the purchase of these commercial territories were in part misappropriated by the Zanu, or that all the apparatchiks of the country took control of such farms as second homes, ruthlessly throwing hundreds of thousands of black agricultural workers into the streets and ruining the productive capacity of the country.

I also could have mentioned the damaging role of the veterans of the war of independence - the war vets, a group to which he belonged, which served and continues to serve as the thugs of the regime. And, finally, that this policy of intimidation and expropriation was still persisting today and was even being directed against the black farmers and black entrepreneurs of Zimbabwe.

But he knew all this. Just as he knew that a large portion of the people were scraping by with great hardship and that the country was on the edge of the abyss because of his Zanu comrades. There was no use in pointing out this state of affairs to him. After all, he lived it every day of his life.

I had understood that attacking the hero of his youth - Bob the liberator - amounted to insulting all the years of sacrifice during which Tendaï, as a freedom fighter, had escaped death many times and lost a considerable number of his comrades. Now he was just trying to find peace with some of his illusions.

How could I claim he was wrong? From personal experience, I found that most of the white people who had been born in Zimbabwe behaved in disgustingly obtuse and racist ways, always nostalgic for the good old days when black people knew how to stay in their place.

And also, whilst there was a certain Anglo-Saxon propaganda that counted the murders caused by the different waves of expropriation which Bob had implemented by the hundreds, a United Nations investigation counted and identified 11 white people who had died (that's 11 too many), but that was in a report that got little attention.

Making an attack on private property a crime justified all the exaggerations and made the whole country seem like a criminal!

And lastly - who was I to explain to a black Zimbabwean how to approach these white Rhodesians - known as 'Rhodies' - who had oppressed them for decades?

During this conversation Tendaï supplied me with a missing piece in my understanding of Bob's vindictive personality. Elaborating on his description of the hypocrisy of Westerners, he brought up an important episode from his hero's career.

In 1994, Bob was on a state visit to the United Kingdom. He was put up in Buckingham Palace and formally received by the Queen herself. This visit was a personal triumph for him since he was knighted by the Queen. Thus, Sir Robert regarded himself as consecrated by his former colonial power.

'However,' Tendaï continued, 'the English knew full well that in 1983 - ten years before then - we Shonas and Ndebeles had settled our scores by ourselves, which had resulted in thousands of civilian deaths.'*

He seemed to pause to contain his anger.

'But for the English it was only some vague story of black people killing each other!'

---

*One should note that Shona-speaking Zimbabweans (75% of the population) along with the Ndebele-speaking Zimbabweans (20% of the population) basically constitute the residents of the country. The main part of this 'settling scores' consisted of a military operation designed by the Zanu, who sent a brigade trained in North Korea into the Ndebele territory with a simple goal: terrorising the people with blind massacres to put an end to any vague notions of political independence. This was also the chance to erase a historical liability: The Ndebeles, breaking with their Zulu cousins in the northeast of what is now South Africa, had taken possession of the southeast of today's Zimbabwe in the 1830s and subjugated the Shona-speaking peoples for decades. The murderous campaign of 1983, in which thousands of innocent Ndebele civilians lost their lives (between 10,000 and 25,000 victims), had an explicit name: Gukurahundi, loosely translated as 'to separate the wheat from the chaff'. Each time we touched upon this sensitive subject, Tendaï would dismiss it with strong words: 'But it was war! You did worse things in your French revolution'.

He continued his explanation of English hypocrisy. I'll sum it up as follows: In 2008 the English revoked Bob's knighthood, using the extreme violence of the elections as an excuse.

To Tendaï, that was not the true reason for the revocation. For the English, it was a chip on their shoulder that white farmers were expelled from the country in the early 2000s. To Tendaï, they had wanted for a long time to make Bob personally pay for the fact that the black people took back their land and that white people lost their lives in the process. And so they humiliated him!

With a move I will never forget, Tendaï spread out his long arms, palms pointing upward, one on each side of his body, imitating the two sides of a scale.

'On the one hand, thousands of black people are killed. That does not stand in the way of a royal knighting. On the other hand, a dozen white people are killed and the title is revoked! Those are the two weights, the two measures!'

I insisted that the terrible bloodbaths during the 2008 elections, where Bob and his men - most notably the war vets - did all they could to retain their power, were enough on their own to bring sanctions to all the Zanu leaders.

Tendaï took a moment to think, evidently performing some type of introspection. He then replied, 'Yes, maybe.'

He seemed taken aback.

'But you should recognise that the English are hypocrites and, as Bob would say, inept!'

The story of the stripped knighthood confirmed my perception of Robert Mugabe as an upset Brit, a rejected lover of the royal throne.

My English colleagues had already brought it to my attention that Bob expressed himself using the most subtle English and that he, furthermore, was recognised as an eminent expert on British heraldry, who could recognise and explain countless coats of arms of the kingdom.

Curiosity drove me to further investigate the few available facts of Bob's life. These revealed to me the traits of a disturbing personality, a man of few words, rather a loner, a man of iron determination and fierceness.

As shown in the writings of Zimbabwean lawyer David Coltart, ever since the years of secrecy Bob led an embittered struggle to achieve power for himself alone.

Bob had physically eliminated everyone who could cast a shadow on his authority, specifically the vice presidents Joshua Nkomo, Simon Muzenda, Joseph Msika, John Nkomo, as well as Zimbabwe's first black general, Solomon Mujuru.

He pulled strings to avoid all direct responsibility for the crimes that were committed. Didn't he claim to be completely uninvolved when the Gukurahundi started because he was on a trip to Asia?

He nurtured an unhealthy jealousy of Nelson Mandela, but one must say that Mandela paid him back. It was he who declared, 'Comrade Bob was shining like a star in the night; then the sun came up.' There's no need to point out who played the role of the sun.

Mugabe made use of all types of intimidation, including poison, to rule by terror. It's not for nothing that he referred to all of his opponents, including those in his camp, as 'little ants that we can crush'.

He was influenced by his two successive wives. His first wife, Sally, who is still worshipped in Zimbabwe today, was a primary school teacher from Ghana, who died before her time in 1992. She tempered Mugabe. Wasn't it she who encouraged him to step down from his position as the head of the country after free elections? His second wife, Grace, was one of his former secretaries and younger than him by 41 years. She was obsessed with power and money all by herself, and she dragged Mugabe to his demise because it was she who brought on his ouster.

He would not hesitate to call upon supernatural worlds which constantly nurtured his mental universe. Like many Zimbabweans, he was convinced that obscure forces influenced the fate of each one of us.

Sick and ageing, he clung to power up to the very end of his reign, under the influence of a manipulative spouse. His 'comrades' who removed him from power were paralysed by the feeling of terror he still inspired in them. They humoured him to the point of denying that a coup d'état had taken place.

I can report on the grotesque character of the palace revolution which ousted Robert Mugabe in November 2017. Whilst Harare was tightly controlled by putschist soldiers and the media was controlled by the army directly, the generals and leaders of the Zanu tried, up to the last minute, to obtain a formal agreement from Mugabe that he was leaving power 'of his own accord'.

The new authorities took absurdity to its extreme, to the point of officially designating the putsch as a 'non coup' and demanding that the diplomatic community do the same.

To tell the truth, this 'non coup' hardly lasted two weeks. It involved neither violence nor victims beyond the definitive exclusion of Grace Mugabe's clan.

Grace Mugabe's clan was known as Generation 40 (G40), the youth organisation of forty-somethings in the Zanu. It opposed the other clan, called Team Lacoste (because of the crocodile logo of Lacoste clothing). It consisted of the Zanu's old guard and was centred around Mnangagwa, whose nickname was 'the crocodile' and who became the country's President after the coup.

For years, Robert Mugabe played one camp against the other as he pleased until Team Lacoste felt it was in danger because Bob was in the process of losing control of G40.

Be that as it may. Even in his aged and diminished state, Bob continued to terrorise all of them with his toxic charisma and his presumed capacity for revenge.

When I mentioned these damning aspects in the career of his idol to Tendaï, I was not prepared for his reaction:

'Well, so what?'

He challenged me to reflect on the perception of historical figures in Europe. Individuals who are considered heroes by this or that European country — he mentioned Henry VIII, Napoleon and Bismarck — were most often regarded as monsters by neighbouring countries.

He maintained that European people have come to terms with their histories and their respective heroes, sometimes to the point of modifying certain truths. He thought it was normal that all important political figures were sainted by the countries they were a part of.

'As for us, we had little choice when picking our heroes. Our only options were those who emerged from the independence movements. Slavery and colonisation had left behind no trace of those women and men who had risen up, resisting the white oppressor.

He thought it unfair that people who did not belong to any specific African nation felt free to pass definitive judgments about national figures, even if they were controversial ones. What Europeans did in Europe amongst Europeans must also be allowed to take place in Africa.

Tendaï relied on the rivalry between Nelson Mandela and Robert Mugabe to bring home his point. Major political figures in Africa are subject to the same animosities and even feelings of hate as their European counterparts. He concluded with this scathing comment:

'Our heroes are black, but that's no reason for them to behave in any way differently from yours!'

I declined from highlighting the jarring approximations in what he said and from pointing out how his analysis downplayed any notion of personal responsibility. I especially appreciated Tendaï's perception of the recent history of African nations, as opposed to the platitudes spread by Africanist ideology.

To him, the history of each African entity supported by the various independence movements was destroyed by the offshore ideology of one Africa, created for the occasion by white people and then by the liberators.

Even though this approach could be open to controversy, I shared Tendaï's conviction that Robert Mugabe's biography was still to be written by and for Zimbabweans. He recognised that the biography was terrible and, he added, romanesque.

'Romanesque?'

Tendaï replied to my question in a categorical manner:

'Bob was passionate about British culture. He made a Shakespearian epic of his life. Bob is our Macbeth, that's it, our Macbeth! Read it again and you will see that there are a lot of parallels with his life!'

I made a certain grimace which Tendaï, who was sometimes very sensitive, took as a sign that I doubted his true knowledge of Shakespeare's plays.

He went on to cite all the tragedies of the great English bard, along with summaries of the main plots. I was stunned; I would have been unable to do the same with the classic plays of our Corneille or Racine!

Trying to regain Tendaï's trust, I followed up, 'In any event, Bob would not have minded seeing his life's story compared to that of an ancient British king.'

I refrained from adding that, come to think of it, the parallel could be extended to the relationship with the people, who very often do not appear in Shakespeare's tragedies. Similarly, Bob considered the people to be mere decoration.

And so the people of Zimbabwe were most often left to fend for themselves, caught up in an exhausting struggle to survive, whilst the country based on the quality of its soil and the richness of its subsoil is one of the richest countries in Africa.

No romanesque biography could gloss over this cruel truth. From this point of view alone, Bob's legacy is damning and his exit pitiable.

The modest string of events that links me to him began with the presentation of my credentials and came to an extravagant epilogue.

One spring day in 2019, I was sitting at an outdoor table of a restaurant in Harare with a friend. Harare offers the very British luxury of a countryside lunch in the very heart of the city. At that very moment I got a call on my mobile. A feeble voice asked to speak with me.

Having trouble understanding the caller, I made him repeat his name twice:

'I am President Mugabe,' he said.

I wondered who this mischievous person might be who wanted to take me for a ride. Out of curiosity, I held out the phone toward my friend, telling him in a mocking tone that it was Bob. When I saw his crumpling countenance, I understood right away that it really was the former President calling.

In a plaintive tone, he asked me to supply him with several crates of Evian water because he and Grace, he specified, drank only that brand and had run out of it since their forced retirement, 18 months ago. I replied that I would make arrangements.

I had the small pleasure of sending a diplomatic cable entitled 'operation Evian water' to have some boxes of this precious liquid shipped from Pretoria.

But once I arrived at my office, I had the instinct to get in touch with my foreign affairs contact whose first reaction was to ask me which number appeared during this strange call. His brutal reaction made it clear to me that this was a State Affair.

An hour later, he called me back and demanded that I not deliver the bottles of Evian to Bob - nor anything else he might ask of me in future. I again had the pleasure of sending out a diplomatic cable, this time entitled 'end of operation Evian water'.

After Bob's misplaced joke on the English affinity for hot water, this was another story which involved water.
Grandeur and decadence.
Robert Mugabe passed away three months later.

Robert and Grace Mugabe

CHAPTER I

CHAPTER II

THE AFRICAN UNION IS A SHAM

*'Africa is really an ocean, a planet unto itself...
We call it Africa, but that is a summary and
convenient simplification. In reality, apart from
the notion of geography, Africa does not exist.'*
Ryszard Kapuscinski, *Ebène*
(published in English as: *The Shadow of the Sun*)

'Africa does not exist, and I'll prove it to you,' Tendaï declared to me, full of self-confidence.

It all started on 26 May 2018 during one of our culinary rituals. Perceiving my gloomy mood, he asked me what had happened to me. I described to him how the Africa Day celebrations the night before at the Rainbow Towers Hotel (formerly Hotel Sheraton) had been even more depressing than usual.

The ambassadors of the 54 African countries had organised a tasting of their special national dishes in the form of a series of buffets. But these were made inaccessible by the numerous Zimbabwean officials who stuck together in tight clusters and were cheerfully stuffing themselves. The highlight of the late evening was the impressive folkloric performance - with the indispensable tams-tams and nude bodies - to celebrate the anniversary of 25 May 1963, the founding day of the Organisation of African Unity, which became the African Union in the 2000s.

The intention may have been laudable, but the result was an interminable diplomatic gala event without soul and, above all, completely disconnected from the people.

Together with all my diplomat colleagues, I had no choice but to participate in this event which was supposed to celebrate 'African unity', amidst the wafts of grease and pastries super-saturated with sugar.

Tendaï was delighted by my description and, as usual, he wanted me to describe in detail what had happened at the reception.

Once his curiosity had been satisfied, he took on a knowing air and said solemnly, 'You weren't celebrating the union of the Africans, but rather the union of the incompetent.'

I asked him to elaborate.

'Incompetence is the only possible explanation for this mystery: Africa is rich, whilst Africans are poor.'

He took one of the atlases I had given him from his black synthetic leather briefcase. As if I didn't understand what he was talking about, Tendaï took on the air of a French notary getting ready to explain the contents of a will, enumerating the wealth of Africa: 90% of the world's platinum reserves, 80% of its diamonds, 60% of its cobalt, 40% of its gold and chromium, etc, not to mention oil, mineral gas, rare earths, etc. 'Furthermore,' he continued, 'it's the perfect continent for solar and wind energy production, and there are also rivers, forests, arable land, etc.'

After producing this long list, Tendaï pointed out that all the maritime commerce and the management of the ports - the link to the rest of the world - was controlled by foreigners and that intra-African trade did not even reach 20% of the total trade volume and, finally, that only one African airline (Ethiopian Airlines) met international standards and that South African Airways was practically bankrupt due to corruption.

At the same time - whilst searching for the page where the data could be found in the atlas - he emphasised with consternation that 37% of Africans lived on less than two dollars per day and 55% on less than 10 dollars per day.

'That's the balance sheet. Incompetent people with the audacity to parade around! Shame on them,' he said, getting passionate.

This was followed by such a dazzling elaboration that it truly impressed me. I took note of what he said. Here are the main points as best as I could record them:

'The African Union is a pipe dream. Why is that? Because Africa does not exist... You heard that right. Africa does not exist - or rather, it is something which you invented and we adopted. Africa is a vast geographical entity, but it can certainly not be reduced to one single entity. Did you know that Africa could contain the surface areas of the United States, China, the European Union, India and almost all of Southeast Asia? Apart from geography, it has no unity. But you never tire of diminishing it in your maps of the world and considering this huge territory to be a self-contained unit. How absurd!

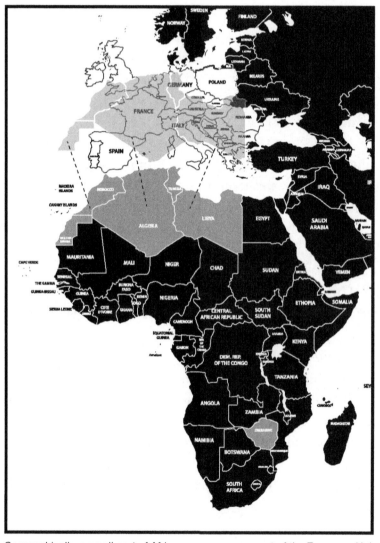

Geographically, a small part of Africa encompasses most of the European Union

Do you think that before you arrived, we 'Africans' - he signalled air quotes with his fingers - thought of ourselves as members of one community? Obviously not! With 1,500 languages, thousands of people with different customs, many cultures and various empires, we were just as different from one another as white people could be different from one another. But you decided to standardise us - first through slavery, taking our humanity away from us, and then through colonisation, by dominating us, and finally through your prejudices, reducing us to *Homo africanus*. Unfortunately, too few traces remain of our histories in the ancient past. So, you and your ethnographers 'reinvented' us. Yet another absurdity! And then there's what you call economic development. Before you came, there was a vast abundance of arable lands, teeming with game, berries, fruits and vegetables. Since there weren't a lot of us and we were spread out across wide expanses, agriculture wasn't always necessary to survive. Some hunting, harvesting, and land management by village elders, and if there was a dispute, it was easy to move along one of our many rivers and find another location. Life wasn't always easy, but it was our life. I read in one of the books you lent me that we were considered underdeveloped because we had not invented the wheel or the plough. But you are forgetting that it is necessity which guides human life: The great Maya and Aztec civilisations didn't need to invent the wheel either. Do you consider them to be underdeveloped as well? That's yet another absurdity! And, above all, there is your obsession with the colour black, that you associate with the threat of the unknown, with evil or with the devil. So when you saw all these African people, black as ebony, the association was automatic. We could be nothing but mysterious, disturbing, wild, depraved and, furthermore, you imagined us to be cut off in darkness since for a long time the interior of the land was hostile to you. And so you decreed that we were 'the black continent' - he once again signalled air quotes - that of magic, savagery and sexual promiscuity. And you called it Africa. As for us, we didn't ask for anything. Yes, I will tell you again: You invented what is called Africa today and its inhabitants, the Africans. That's absurd and criminal!'

I remained speechless in the face of such barely contained anger. Tendaï had lost his aloofness. He had an uncertain gaze, a sagging face and falling shoulders, as if overcome by an immense fatigue.

He had just revealed an intimate part of himself, a burning pain that, it seemed, nothing could soothe. I was shaken by this intimacy, as sudden as it was unprecedented. Tendaï was not just a bright intellectual. He lived his convictions in real life to the point of feeling the pain and suffering in his soul.

I signalled to the waiter to bring us two beers. Tendaï drank his up in one gulp. I chose to remain quiet whilst he regained his composure.

At first he clammed up. He opened up little by little and then made an unusual gesture. He extended his hand and placed it softly on my shoulder. Looking me right in the eye, he said in a terse yet warm tone, 'Thank you for listening to me.'

And for the first time, he revealed personal information about himself:

'In prison, I earned a master's degree in the history of civilisation and - after independence - a second master's in sociology.'

He paused, removed his hand from my shoulder and continued with a friendly smile, 'I didn't do as well as Bob, who got three master's degrees during his 11 years in prison.'

Tendaï had just opened a breach which I hoped to use to enter into a relationship that was not simply intellectual, but he left me no time for this. He continued with great clarity.

'Don't get the idea that I'm a nostalgic hankering back to a time when African people were authentic. Many black intellectuals glorify the time before white people came. I don't believe in this type of reverie on tradition for a single second. It's nonsense! We don't really know what happened before, so what's the use in dreaming? I'm just talking about what happened since you broke into our world and the consequences we have suffered, even after independence.'

I assumed that he would now want to discuss how Europeans artificially redrew the borders of African countries and created new ones. This was indeed the case, but his approach to the subject went against the grain of conventional wisdom.

'On all continents it was always the winners who drew the borders. Most of the time they did this in an artificial way because they cut up the territories to suit their own interests. So there was no reason to think that we, the losers, would be an exception to this ancient rule of humankind. Indeed, the Europeans set the borders in a manner contrary to any common sense, without asking our opinion on the matter.

Well, it's been that way for decades now and we've been living with it. Better yet, I'd say that with time, a sense of belonging to this or that nation has set in. You live in Zimbabwe. Go tell someone from Zimbabwe that he or she is the same as a person from Zambia or Malawi or even South Africa. See how much

they will love you for it! The Africa Cup of Nations in football -
that tells you a lot more than the 'Union of the Incompetent'....'

His lively and mocking expression had returned. With his
head held high and his shoulders straightened, he perked up and
continued his train of thought.

'There are as many differences between someone from
Senegal or Malawi or Eritrea or Angola as there are between a
Finn and a Greek. All the African nations are different from each
other. It's just like in Europe. No European nation is the same
as another European nation. So stop saying 'Africa, the black
continent'. You don't say 'Asia, the yellow continent' or 'Europe,
the white continent'. That wouldn't make any sense. But, no, you
still have your strange obsession with blackness. And the worst of
it is that we still believe in a sort of fraternity amongst us because
we have black skin. That's absurd again!'

He paused briefly.

'Even after the various independences, you were never
willing to take into account the irreducible specificities of each
liberated African nation. But you Europeans would not confuse the
nation-building processes of Italy with those of The Netherlands,
for example. So treat us the same! You should consider each
African country with its own political and cultural characteristics
and not reduce it to a vague subcategory of some ill-defined entity.'

He paused to take a breath.

'And on our end we must also stop talking about Africa
in global terms! All the issues of constructing a state ruled by
law, of respecting political freedom, of economic development, of
governance, of cultural imprinting, of the creation of the social
contract, etc - are these issues the same everywhere in Africa? Of

course not. So it's urgent to identify precisely the many shapes that Africa takes.'

Tendaï once again drew his parallel to the situation in Europe.

'You in France consider yourselves to be French first and foremost. And you stay French, even if some of you - and not all, if I understand correctly - consider yourselves to be Europeans. Is that right?'

I confirmed it was, and he continued.

'So it's the same for us. There is no country that calls itself Africa - and there are even fewer people who identify as Africans. These artificial ideas are contaminating us.'

He searched for words, lost in his thoughts. I dared not spur him on. At last, he continued.

'I have stated that Africa does not exist, but I'm convinced that it could exist. We have to free ourselves of this false 'black brotherhood'. He surely must have read this in the book which I lent him written by Axelle Kabou, the Franco-Senegalese expert in development. 'We must turn strictly to defending our interests. Not those of Africa, but those of each nation which constitutes it. Just like you did for the European Union. You don't really love each other amongst Europeans, but you became aware that you could manage much better by each of you defending your own interests if the pie were shared. By becoming more and more French, German and Italian, you became more and more European. That's the path one has to follow. There is no need to reject everything that comes from you!'

His face lit up with a mocking smile. Then he continued speaking in a more sombre tone.

'With the 'Union of the Incompetent' we are not ready to take this path. We all have internalised the story of skin colour as our identitarian flag to such a degree that we are even more tied down. These stories of 'brother' and of 'sister' on the basis of our dark epidermis have just become intolerable to me.'

I interrupted him. He couldn't just throw by the wayside the enthusiasm surrounding the idea of African unity that was spreading across the continent before and even more after the independences. Even if the results were slim, this movement finally brought pride and dignity. And even today, one cannot deny that the idea of African unity is still present in the minds of the peoples of Africa.

'Actually,' I tried to explain, 'calling oneself African is just the same as calling oneself European. It's a horizon to reach for, involving the idea of a shared destiny.'

I couldn't see why he objected so adamantly to such an ambition.

Again, he took his time before formulating his answer.

'It's simple. Today this is preventing us from being ourselves. Here is what I mean. In its day African Unity was an acceptable aspiration - even if the idea of unity was directly inspired by European cultural hegemony. Recall the 'négritude' movement of Senghor, Damas and Césaire. But, today, it has become a pernicious ideology. All these stories - of the awakening of Africa, this dream of Mother Africa, which African-American journalist Keith Richburg called 'black Walhalla', all the incoherencies of Pan-Africanism that were not founded in anything concrete, this illusion of the continent's cultural unity - all these might have kindled hope, but for decades now, Mother Africa has mostly been the mother of suffering, disillusionment and hopelessness for the Africans. I am not speaking out against being African as a concept - far from it. I'm just speaking out against the Africanist ideology which brought us so much harm.'

From his synthetic leather briefcase, he took out the book *The Invention of Africa* by Valentin-Yves Mudimbe, which I had never heard of until then.

Tendaï started off with a joke: 'To tell you the truth, despite my master's degree in sociology, I'm not sure I've understood everything in this book. I had to start over several times.'

His honesty was as disarming as ever. He continued on.

'There's a passage I'd like to read to you since it expresses far better than I could the traps of Africanness. Mudimbe cites a philosopher from Benin, Paulin J. Hountondji:

'We had to start by demythifying Africanness, by reducing it to a factual statement - the simple and per se neutral fact of belonging to Africa - while dissipating the mystic halo of values that have been arbitrarily grafted onto this fact by the ideologies of African identity. It was necessary to return the spectacle of our history to its original simplicity in order to conceptualise its complexity, and then, to conceptualise the richness of African traditions, we had to resolutely impoverish the concept of Africa; we had to strip it of all its ethical, religious, philosophical, and political, etc connotations with which a long anthropological tradition has burdened it and whose most visible effect was to limit the horizon, to close history prematurely.'

Sensitive as I was to this line of thinking, I felt that we were off on yet another tangent on the roots of Africanness. I thus took the liberty of adding some direction to the conversation to avoid getting lost in the meanderings of muddled thinking.

'Very well then. What should be done? You reject the illusion of the so-called authentic African traditions — and I understand you — and yet, at the same time, you pan the Africanist screen put up by the leaders and elites. I admit that I don't quite understand.'

He held Mudimbe's book in my direction.

'Here you go. This is for you. It's a gift. It contains some interesting thoughts.'

Tendaï had just given me a gift — and not just any gift but a book! Knowing that books are luxury goods in Zimbabwe, I appreciated the value of this act. It was all dog-eared from being read and reread. He couldn't have given me a more meaningful gift.

Grateful, I stuttered:

'Thank you — thank you from the bottom of my heart.'

In response he simply got up and invited me to follow him: 'Come now, we've been sitting for a long time. Let's take a few steps.'

He led me to the plant nursery which spread out on the other side of the road, right across from the cafeteria of the Baybridge supermarket, where we were sitting. We walked side by side in the freshness of the potted ferns, which were lined up along a dirt path.

'You really are French. For you, 1 + 1 must equal 2, but in the lives of people, this sum is rather 1.5 or 2.3… But I won't dodge your question. What to do? I'm not claiming to have a ready-made answer. I just have the strong conviction that we must live in the present of each African nation. Look, in Zimbabwe we have ancient traditions even if they have been somewhat forgotten or turned into folklore. We experienced war amongst ourselves, the Shonas and the Ndebeles; we experienced slavery; we experienced colonisation; we suffered to gain our independence; today we face great hardships. Well, we are the result of all this history. It is ours. I would even say that we are this history. And I would go further. We also are the legend that your ethnographers construed about our past, all those intellectual constructs about our tribal life and our so-called animist practices - everything your ethnographers made up since they didn't understand what they were looking at. Well, we are also that! In short, we should see ourselves as history, and its trials have shaped us. We must reappropriate everything that makes us who we are today. Do you follow me?'

I nodded, since I was starting to understand what Tendaï was getting at.

'It's not just about coming to terms with one's past but also about reappropriating it fully and in its entirety - the good and the bad, the suffering and the successes, the glory and the decline - and recognising one's role as a legitimate heir who continues this story. We must put an end to our complexes and our dependence. We are the product of everything that has happened to us, and we should be proud of it!

That's what you did in Europe. Now it's up to us - to each African nation - to do it. Yes, I'm saying every African nation because the countries of Africa each have different histories even with slavery and colonisation.'

He paused.

'The young generations can change things. At any rate, that's what I'm hoping for. And then, only then, once all the African nations feel whole as they are, may we be able to speak of the African Union. Since you are an heir to Descartes, I could summarise my thoughts in two logical steps: first to renationalise the history of each country in Africa and then to make our collective future colour-blind.'

He walked me to my car. He declined my offer to drop him off anywhere he wanted — he must not have liked the idea of being transported in a large car with a diplomatic license plate.

He thanked me for lunch and left. Long ago, I had given up asking how I could reach him on a mobile phone — the syndrome of the underground fighter forever... He would get in touch with me again, as usual.

I had barely sat down in my car when I rushed to jot down Tendaï's points, first of all to learn from them but also to be well prepared for our next lunch.

I was impressed. I really wished there were an honorific form of address in English as there is in French: Tendaï was a true gentleman, an honest man, surely full of contradictions, but aren't we all? On the other hand, he had a healthy curiosity and refused to accept predigested ideas. He was somebody who critically questioned his time.

I saw that he wasn't rich and must have been in need of a lot of things. How could I offer to help him without offending him? I did not know.

All countries in Africa must have scores of people like Tendaï, who are discreet and modest. How can they be reached? How can their existence be acknowledged? How can one get around the leaden ideological trap of the regimes in power? How can one get around the dogmas of the African intellectuals so beloved by the media?

Once more, I left our meeting with more questions than answers but with some comfort. Tendaï was right. It was up to the young people of Africa to take the reins. And, also, he had presented this proposition which seemed more than relevant to me: 'To renationalise the history of each country in Africa and then to make our collective future colour-blind'. Truly a horizon to reach for!

CHAPTER II

CHAPTER III

THE DENIGRATION OF HISTORY

'The major accomplishment of the West has been to conceptualise other people and create meaning about them...'

Sami Tchak

Le Continent du Tout et du presque Rien
(The Continent of Everything and Almost Nothing)

In the book Tendaï gave me as a gift, *The Invention of Africa*, Congolese philosopher Valentin-Yves Mudimbe lists, in what he calls the colonial library, the totality of the representations and the texts that have, in the West, shaped what Africa has become in our collective imagination.

The author details how the European conquerors — seeking to constrain and then dominate — pulled out all the stops. One of the cruelest ruses was to deny the historic roots and the identity of each people that they wanted to subjugate. Knowing this is one thing, experiencing it quite another.

That's what I encountered first-hand in Zimbabwe as I sought to find out about the history of that country.

When you leave Harare heading due south, you find yourself on a straight road, bordered on both sides by an endless savanna with a sparse canopy of trees. For 300 kilometres, you won't come across a living soul, other than herds of baboons who pay no attention to your passing by.

You will then reach the small city of Masvingo, whose urban architecture and right-angled main street grid bring to mind the mushrooming cities at the time of the American westward expansion. This is no coincidence because it is the oldest European-settled colony in Zimbabwe. At that time - in 1890 - it was named Fort Victoria.

There are many traces of colonial Rhodesia, so many nostalgic signs of a time gone by that refuses to end - the main street that is still wide enough for an eight-horse buggy to turn around, the little Victoria Hotel which is dominated by the relief portrait of the English queen; locomotives from the early 20th century that can be seen here and there.

In the deadening heat of day - Masvingo is one of Zimbabwe's hottest cities - you are desperately looking for a sign that shows the direction to the archaeological ruins of Great Zimbabwe. It's no use. There aren't any signs. You've got to ask the locals, who like everywhere else in the country - even the remotest of places - will always be ready to help you.

After 30 kilometres, you reach a maze of small mountains that extend as far as the eye can see, to the border with Mozambique, which is about 200 kilometres away. You encounter countless variations of grey and green in this very hilly landscape, which consists of granite rocks surrounded by dense plant life. You soon get the feeling you've entered a special world.

You have now arrived at the entrance to the site. In the distance, atop a long overhang, you make out walls of a spectacular height made of carved stone. A steep, narrow, rocky path, sometimes forming natural obstacles, gives access to one of the entrances, a solid fortified portico.

Those who have had the chance to visit the Cathar castles in southern France will spot a striking resemblance. It's the same method of assembling stones without mortar, the same type of walls whose buttresses are more than 4 metres thick and which are over ten meters high.

This resemblance is even more troubling since the construction of the Cathar castles occurred at about the same time as that of Great Zimbabwe. Both are dated around the 12th and 13th centuries.

Zimbabwe means 'stone house'.

Don't expect too much of your local guide. He'll explain to you that *zimbabwe* means 'stone house' in the Shona language. You'll also learn that after independence this site lent its name to the country and that the falcon-shaped rock that towers over the place was the symbol of the kings of the time and the soapstone bird sculpture appears on the national flag today.

The guide will not spare you vulgar comments about the kings who had at least 200 wives or hide his delight in explaining to you that some of the little monkeys - male vervets - that won't let go of you during your visit have electric blue genitals because this attracts the females.

That's just about it. We don't really know who these kings were; exactly how big their territory was; which people they reigned over; what their social organisation was; what their rites and beliefs were; what languages they spoke; nor how their vast trade network was organised - shards of Chinese and Persian porcelain are scattered throughout the site.

We can only surmise that this trade was encouraged by the considerable goldmines of the region, which are still operated today. You cannot count on the modest hut that serves as a museum to get information. It is routinely closed to the public due to the lack of maintenance and electricity.

From the top of these impressive walls you can admire another building below, which is just as spectacular. It is called the Great Enclosure and was the imposing residence of the queen and the princes - a hypothesis rather than an established fact - as well as a web of stone paths, formerly covered with canopies of stone arches that have collapsed. You don't need to be an archeologist to surmise that as far as the eyes can see the countless mounds are so many archaeological sites waiting to be investigated.

The soapstone bird sculpture features on the flag.

An exciting yet frustrating visit that at least proves wrong any peremptory affirmations that sub-Saharan Africa kept itself completely separated from the history of the world.

I was later to learn that the only written mention of this site came from two handwritten letters from a Portuguese traveller in the 16th century who had visited the place at a time when the decline of the kingdom was already well underway. At its height the kingdom seems to have extended from Transvaal in South Africa to a vast coastal region on the Indian ocean including the Zambezi valley and the mountains of eastern Zimbabwe. In this immense territory one could count nearly 600 sites with buildings related to those of Great Zimbabwe.

There are only few studies which propose at least some hypotheses concerning this civilisation: a powerful and very populous African kingdom with an advanced building technology which was capable of producing beautiful gold jewellery and was linked to far-away worlds. All of this is comparable in many ways — except for the presence of written documents — to our European Middle Ages.

I noticed a cultural resemblance between the people of this kingdom and those of the Celtic world in Europe, mostly found in France and the United Kingdom. They were part of a sophisticated civilisation and are poorly known since the Celtic druids only favoured the oral tradition. Perhaps this was also the case with the shamans of Great Zimbabwe.

I was so fascinated that I returned to this site a dozen times, as if magnetised by its spiritual power.

The kingdom of Great Zimbabwe is thought to have collapsed starting in the 16th century under the weight of significant overpopulation, coupled with multiple successive droughts and perhaps also political problems that we are not aware of, as was the case at the same time and for the same reasons with the fall of the Maya empire on the Yucatan peninsula.

Then, for over three centuries, the site was forgotten by humankind.

In the second half of the 19th century, British adventurer Cecil Rhodes - the founder of the South African diamond conglomerate De Beers - and his underlings arrived in the region. They were so impressed by the ruins that they preferred the Biblical hypothesis - which matched their literal understanding of the Bible - that these fortresses had to be of Semitic origin and certainly could not have been built by people with black skin. In fact, during the Rhodesian period it was a crime punishable by prison to claim that Great Zimbabwe was built by black people.

It was a very fashionable view amongst the philosophers of colonisation at the time that Semitic peoples (Jews, Arabs and Phoenicians) had come from the North to the South - from the banks of the Red Sea or along the Nile, into the heart of southern Africa. This vague theory caused powerful ethnic divides, which underlay appalling human tragedies, particularly in the Great Lakes region.

The numerous goldmines around this site gave rise to crazy fantasies at the end of the 19th century. They were considered to be the work of a Near Eastern civilisation. The idea quickly spread that Great Zimbabwe could only be the epicentre of King Salomon's true realm and of his inexhaustible wealth.

A popular book endorsing this vision was *King Solomon's Mines* by Rider Haggerd in the late 19th century. The vision was further propagated by film adaptions in the 20th century: the first in 1937 with Paul Robeson, the second in 1950 with Deborah Kerr and Stewart Granger, whose plots took place somewhere in Africa, and the 1986 film *Allan Quatermain and the Lost City of Gold* with Richard Chamberlain and Sharon Stone, which was filmed … in Zimbabwe!

At this site, the white Rhodesians took this denial of a civilisation built by black people even further in the 1950s. They rerouted the river that flowed at the foot of Great Zimbabwe, bulldozed the ground for several square kilometres around the spur and built a golf course at the foot of the citadel.

Even today certain white people who live in Zimbabwe can't fathom that black people could have built such an expansive kingdom.

When I again had the chance to meet Tendaï for the customary grilled chicken and authentically chemical-laden Fanta, I enthusiastically told him all about my encounter with Great Zimbabwe.

'Dominating us wasn't enough for them. They also had to erase any trace of our history,' Tendaï sighed.

He reminded me that this was more or less the colonisers' first reflex throughout all of sub-Saharan Africa. For example, the sophisticated artistic developments in the Kingdom of Benin were first attributed to Portuguese influence, the Yoruba statuary technique to Egyptian influence, etc.

Some time later he lent me another book - worn down by heavy use - so I could get an idea of precolonial sub-Saharan Africa. It was *The Lost Cities of Africa* by Basil Davidson.

Despite all this, I was again bothered by Tendaï's tendency to ignore his government's responsibility in not giving value to the historical sites of the country.

I mentioned to him that there had been no substantial archaeological research around Great Zimbabwe in the last 40 years. It was as if history were cut short to only begin with independence. It's hard to blame the coloniser for this.

Tendaï acknowledged this but chalked it up to a basic cultural difference between us. Westerners were too fond of dissecting the past and examining the secrets of the ancients without any modesty, whilst the Shona, for their part, preferred to fear their ancestors, honour their souls and protect themselves from invisible powers. That's why poking around at Great Zimbabwe could not be scheduled until an otherworldly sign authorised it.

I wasn't quite convinced, but I preferred not to push my point. It wasn't until much later that I understood what he meant.

To Tendaï this mutual lack of understanding was not the key element in the relationship between black people and Westerners. In his view, it was only the consequence of another process, namely the 'incomplete annihilation'. This is what he called the Western colonisation of Africa.

The incomplete annihilation of the African people - just saying the phrase curdles my blood - was for Tendaï the true aim of colonisation since, as he maintained, to colonise was first and foremost to destroy.

His analysis, at this point, upset all established presuppositions.

He affirmed to me that between the mid-19th century and the 1930s, at the height of colonisation, one third of the population of black Africa was massacred either through military conquest or as part of the occupation or by diseases brought by the Europeans. His affirmation seemed plausible, but I have not been able to verify, given the absence of uncontested documentation.

Tendaï was convinced that if the European colonists could have come to Africa in larger numbers, they would have done without black labour and would not have hesitated to inflict the same fate on the Africans as they had done to the Native Americans, stealing their land and erasing their history.

To him, a complete genocide was avoided because of the difficult conditions of access to the African continent - the deserts in the North and South, the strong winds sweeping the coasts, the fauna which is often hostile, the vegetation which is impenetrable in many places and, finally, and most important of all, malaria. Synthetic quinine was not on the market until 1944. There are good reasons why Africa became known as 'the tomb of the white man'.

'You see,' he went on, 'those unfortunate native peoples of America came across the same Europeans that we did. But they had the bad luck of living in a place that was easily accessible. And so they were 'genocided away'!'

He could have added that white Americans in the United States not only systematically massacred the natives but also turned this genocide into a national epic in the form of blockbuster Westerns.

Bitter and disillusioned, Tendaï concluded with a macabre twist:

'In the end, we black people had better luck because we could be enslaved!'

The word had been uttered: slave, the one that I could not say in front of him, no doubt because I felt shame. That day neither he nor I wished to pursue our dialogue on such a painful subject.

Some days later, Tendaï let me know that he was ready to talk with me about difficult subjects without having our discussion turn into an ideological confrontation. I jumped at the opportunity and asked if it would be OK to discuss slavery. He consented.

I told him about my surprise about how little information was available in Zimbabwe concerning the hateful slave trade. He confirmed to me that for many Zimbabweans the time of slavery appeared vague and uncertain. In Harare there were neither a museum, nor a memorial nor any events hosted about the subject. Apart from some overly general books, nothing referred back to this barbarous period.

This situation was even worse in Malawi, the neighbouring country where I also represented France.

The region near Lake Malawi was at the heart of a major slave trading network that spanned from the Congo basin in the West to the Persian Gulf in the East, passing through Zanzibar, yet nothing made it easy for Malawians interested in the history of their country to learn how the network was organised.

I learned about the extent of the ravages of slavery from reading thousands of pages of letters by the Scottish explorer David Livingstone.

On his first expedition in 1856, Livingstone encountered a densely populated, friendly region around Lake Malawi with a rich and diverse agriculture. A few years later, on his second expedition, he only saw desolation, abandoned villages, corpses along the road, and long lines of chained slaves in this same location. He emphasised that it was always black Africans, accompanied by Arab merchants, who devoted themselves to this dreadful bloodletting.

Opening up this tragic period to serious historical scrutiny amounts to disclosing that certain Malawians of today are the direct descendants of slave traders who were very active in selling into slavery those who were to become their fellow citizens decades later. This certainly applies to Malawi - and to a lesser extent to Zimbabwe.

In other words, it would amount to Malawian society finally facing up to the fact that some of its citizens were involved in the slave trade. But civil peace has its price, so it is easier to accuse foreign slave traders, be they Arab or Portuguese.

Contrary to others, Tendaï did not deny that slavery was already a part of the picture in sub-Saharan Africa before white people burst in. It was organised by black notables and Arab merchants.

But he was stunned by the numbers I presented to him - in fact these were only estimates that I had attempted to bring together.

The internal slave trade (amongst Africans) was not as 'family-oriented and good-natured' as some African intellectuals present it today. Several millions of people seem to have been involved (there are no reliable data). Some sources talk about ten million uprooted people; the trans-Saharan and oriental slave trade was organised by Arab merchants and is said to have involved deporting five to 12 million people (this discrepancy shows the extent of our ignorance). To this day, no Arab countries have assumed responsibility for this. Finally, there was the transatlantic slave trade (which is better documented). It was piloted primarily by the Portuguese, the English and the French. It is said to have removed 12 to 14 million people from their land.

Tendaï mentioned to me that these numbers did not take into account the slaves who perished during their transport from the hinterlands to the coast.

According to David Livingstone, for every one slave who arrived, three slaves died during transport. For some routes, he claimed that the ratio was one to five.

Tendaï thought that it wasn't just up to white people to examine this past and to take responsibility for all aspects of this tragedy. According to him, this is above all the job for the Africans. He was alarmed that we cannot state, or even try to state, the names of the vast majority of these wretched victims who were dehumanised and sold like merchandise.

He suspected it would be very difficult, but he thought we should at least find the names of the clans, the tribes, the villages, and the places - everything that could make it possible to date, to locate and to trace these trails of death in time and space.

He complained about the common generalisations about 'black slavery' that are so often expressed. Just like the concept of Africa, this is another catch-all phrase that hides the intimate reality of the women and men whose individual memory we must honour.

His remark brought to mind the extensive work done by Jewish Holocaust survivors: naming the victims to make them exist as human beings.

I promised Tendaï that I would give him the contact details of the African academics and associations that work in this area - especially in western Africa. I never found out whether he contacted them.

In a perfect world one could imagine that the big European and Arab slave-trading countries would finance a large programme led by African historians who would try to identify by name to the extent possible the women and men who were dehumanised. They would make use of all the archives, travel narratives and oral traditions and conduct extensive field work.

We are far away from this.

At the current time, people still present to us the Île de Gorée in Senegal as a major location where West African slaves boarded ships departing for America. But the truth is quite different. There were slaves who passed through Gorée, but its rocky coast definitely does not allow for the intensive slave trade that supposedly took place there.

The explanation for the mythical status of Gorée can perhaps be found in the visual configuration of the site. As tourists approach a building gate at the end of a funnel-shaped corridor, they can see the Atlantic opening out in the exact direction of America, thousands of kilometres away. All of this is very symbolic.

House of slaves - Île de Gorée

Gorée is a place of symbolic value. But what would we think about a visually striking fake extermination camp to better illustrate the Holocaust?

At our next lunch, Tendaï confronted me head on with a blunt question: 'Why are white people convinced they belong to a superior civilisation?'

My attempts at an explanation were so vague that even today I still feel embarrassed about it. Luckily, in such cases, at least I know of a solution: enlightenment through books. So I gave him the book *The History of White People* by African-American historian Nell Irvin Painter. The first consequence of this gift was that I didn't see Tendaï for one month.

When we met again, he told me that he had left his church – one of those countless Protestant congregations whose name I have forgotten. To quote Tendaï, this was because 'Ms Painter opened up my eyes'.

He summed up what he had gathered from this major academic work. The main theorists of racialist thought appeared in Lower Saxony (today part of Germany) at the end of the 18th century in the city of Göttingen. One of these figures, named Johann Friedrich Blumenbach, ranked the human races with white people in first place because, according to him, racial superiority expresses itself as beauty and white people were the ones he considered most beautiful. Tendaï did not understand why Caucasians - especially Caucasian women - would have been considered the most aesthetically advanced.

What especially attracted Tendaï's attention is that Lower Saxony under the leadership of the princes of Hanover was where the English kings came from. So it was natural for the elite of the Saxon country to be culturally and intellectually very closely linked to the British Empire.

In the mid-19th century, English writer Thomas Carlyle expanded on Blumenbach's theories by praising the superior merit of the Saxon race and advocating for racial purity. This ideology then spread to the United States where the myth of Anglo-Saxon superiority permanently took root.

Sounding like a detective who has solved a case, Tendaï told me in a knowing tone, 'And so when the British came here at the end of the 19th century, they had their minds full of this nonsense. The 'Rhodies' are the monstrous children of these thought criminals, like all white supremacists.'

Of course, I had read these passages in Painter's book, but I did not remember them as precisely as he did. Especially when Tendaï needled me with a mocking smile, 'And do you know what Carlyle called the French?'

I had no idea. When I couldn't answer, he went on, 'A nation of monkeys.'

That judgment was in line with Thomas Carlyle's writing, poisonous and contemptuous.

It bothered me that Tendaï thought these theories were uniquely an Anglo-Saxon phenomenon. So I took it upon myself to let him know that French people were also involved in the race craze of the period. He asked me for names of writers and carefully noted the spelling. The only one I could think of was Arthur de Gobineau. I promised to make him a more comprehensive list.

I also explained to him that the important thing was that by theorising the inferiority of the black race, the Anglo-Saxons and the French were seeking above all to provide legal and philosophical legitimacy to slavery as it was ending and colonisation as it was beginning.

'That's true,' Tendaï replied, 'but it was still Protestant culture in which the conviction was born that black people are members of an inferior race and mixed-race people are demonic creatures.'

Tendaï then denounced everything that could be closely or remotely related to the Protestant religion. I had to rein him in by mentioning Catholic culture, which is definitely different but pernicious just the same.

For example, French colonisation was opposed to the idea of racial hierarchies. However, it was just as obsessed with the idea of universality for all people. 'I dominate you to elevate you to my status' was the name of the game. Racial mixing was not disapproved of, but it was ambiguous — 'Loving your neighbour, even through rape, opens the door to civilisation'. Both cultures engendered colonial systems, one as revolting as the other.

Tendaï closed this long chapter of our dialogue by bowing his head, overwhelmed, and with a dismayed expression. As he raised his head again, he looked squarely into my eyes and murmured in a weary voice: 'White people!'

Our European meat grinder gave its fullest in sub-Saharan Africa with the 'industrialisation' of slavery, with extreme colonisation, with the devaluation of traditional ways of life and with an ever more intense grip on the economy.

I whole-heartedly share Tendaï's conviction that the youth of Africa - luckily it is in the majority - will end up taking possession of this heavy heritage.

We must hope that it doesn't get lost in the false intoxication of a return to 'African authenticity' but that it will instead fight for the peoples of Africa to be considered subjects in their own right and not objects under guardianship, both inside and outside of Africa.

We must move forward and see what the future can hold, but we must also free ourselves of certain things we got wrong in the past. Victimisation is one of those obstacles which penalise both individuals and society, not only in Zimbabwe but also more widely in sub-Saharan Africa.

On a related note, when Tendaï one day brought up the subject of the victim status of Africa, I reminded him of the unfortunate history of Liberia and the tragic fate of Ethiopia, the only two countries in Africa that were not colonised.

CHAPTER IV

THE DAMAGING EFFECTS OF INTERNATIONAL AID

*'Africans are the only people on earth
to believe their development can be
handled by people other than themselves.'*

Axelle Kabou

Et si l'Afrique refusait le développement?
(What if Africa refuses development?)

Professionals in humanitarian aid and experts in development aid have created an abstract image of Africa as a place where people - the hypothetical African people - live who are in desperate need of international aid.

With major mobilisation campaigns and media coverage, they have created the idea in Western public opinion that all of Africa is in dire need of aid.

Amongst these professional 'helpers' we find a mix of the major agencies of the UN, government agencies of Nordic countries, the EU, NGOs from around the world and private and public charities, not to mention banks and specialised financial institutions. In short, there is a vast conglomerate with its procedures, its jargon and, of course, a certain propensity to compete with one another.

To get a better grasp of them, we should take the perspective of the African beneficiaries, who give them just one name, the 'donors', that is 'the ones who pay'. Clear and simple.

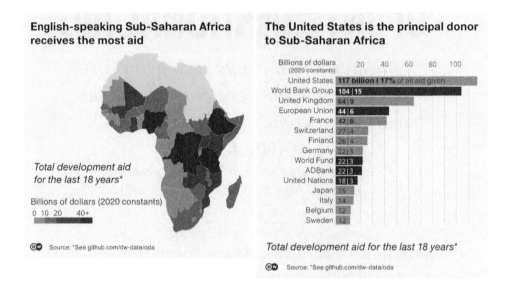

English-speaking Sub-Saharan Africa receives the most aid

Total development aid for the last 18 years*

Billions of dollars (2020 constants)
0 10 20   40+

Source: *See github.com/dw-data/oda

The United States is the principal donor to Sub-Saharan Africa

Billions of dollars (2020 constants)	20	40	60	80	100
United States	117 billion I 17% of all aid given
World Bank Group	104 | 15
United Kingdom	64 | 9
European Union	44 | 6
France	42 | 6
Switzerland	27 | 4
Finland	26 | 4
Germany	22 | 3
World Fund	22 | 3
ADBank	22 | 3
United Nations	18 | 3
Japan	15
Italy	14
Belgium	12
Sweden	12

*Total development aid for the last 18 years**

Source: *See github.com/dw-data/oda

From 2004 to 2022, Africa received 805 billion dollars in public development aid, compared to the Marshall Plan where Europe received 13 billion dollars in loans from 1948 to 1952. In 2022 dollars this was the equivalent of about 170 billion dollars (source: DW-data). According to the World Bank, 90% of the poorest people on earth will be living in Africa in 2030.

But we must carefully distinguish the humanitarian donors from the development donors. They are close cousins. But one type mobilises in emergencies and has many times proven its capacity to save human lives, whilst the others have a mid- and long-term perspective, convinced that they are bringing the tools necessary for economic development.

Donors are not just passive. They can also get involved in areas which matter to them such as sustainable development, fighting climate change, preserving biodiversity and protecting LGBTQ minorities. Donors find local networks in order to promote their values.

Thus, looked at from a distance, the dynamic between the donors and the beneficiaries seems rather virtuous. Is that still the case when we look at it up close?

Not really. I was about to be confronted with many learning opportunities.

First there was the meeting hosted by the EU representative which brought together all the ambassadors from EU countries posted to Harare with the Zimbabwean organisations that worked under the 'European umbrella' (a term developed in Brussels) in the region of Bulawayo, the second largest city in the country, located in the Ndebele-speaking area.

It was early in 2017. I had just arrived in Zimbabwe and I was thrilled to be meeting Zimbabweans who were involved in civic struggles, especially alongside European colleagues. In fact, this trip of several days, which covered a distance of 450 km from the capital, felt like participating in an excursion organised by the Erasmus student exchange programme.

Only Her Majesty's representative, a woman from Wales, spoiled the visit a bit with her hypocritical and superficial attitude which reminded me of all the hackneyed British stereotypes. Luckily, she was replaced a few months later by an Englishwoman, who turned out to be open and sincerely European.

The highlight of the stay was to be the plenary meeting, hosted by the EU representative, in which the charities and Zimbabwean NGOs were to engage.

Lawyers, journalists, academics, instructors, and ordinary citizens had organised themselves in small structures financed by the EU. Each one focused on a particular topic, ranging from women's rights to legal assistance by way of the fight against police violence and, of course, the acknowledgment of the massacre of tens of thousands of Ndebele-speaking civilians in the 1980s by the regime of Robert Mugabe.

The plenary meeting started with an explanation of the role of the so-called 'umbrella structure'. The 'umbrella' was tasked with coordinating all these organisations and the 'umbrella' found itself clearly authorised to 'represent civil society' by the EU representatives present at this meeting.

Was the structure elected, designated or self-proclaimed? Did it speak in the name of someone or something and under what mandate? What type of civil society was it working toward? So many questions were left without answers.

This was followed by almost three hours of an exhausting medley of technocratic EU newspeak. Here are some glorious examples: high-performance reporting, inclusive process, open ecosystem, transparent governance, implementation process, citizen foresight, mid-term review, and, of course, monitoring this and monitoring that...

On the one hand, the charities justified their use of the funds, as branch offices of an international company might do when dealing with their headquarters, doggedly requesting increased resources. On the other hand, the EU representatives scupulously attended to ticking all the bureaucratic boxes which Brussels had defined as proof of an exemplary cooperation.

However, the women and men from Zimbabwe that we had spoken with in smaller circles during the meetings were very good people who struggled day by day to further their causes and, doing that, took all the risks.

They had simply adapted to the European verbiage to be able to finance their existence as an oppositional force.

On another note, some time after this Erasmus trip, the representatives of the World Food Programme (WFP) invited me and the American ambassador, who was an African American, to come see how they were helping the poorest and most remote villages in the very south of the country, right next to the border with Mozambique. They had a clear objective: to obtain continued funding from the two donors, the Americans and the French.

By training the villagers to control the nearby water flow and to create small dams, WFP had indeed obtained spectacular results.

At long last, the residents of three villages could leave poverty behind by growing diverse crops and also using fish farming as a new source of income.

But it was really not necessary to ask the hundreds of villagers that met us for the occasion to greet us with the rumbling of drums, folkloric dances, exuberant singing and costumes fitting the occasion. There was no need for them to be dressed in their traditional clothes to convince two Westerners to add more money to the pot.

I felt embarrassed for my African American colleague and impatiently awaited the end of this strange ceremony staged by the welcoming committee with the support of WFP.

I had hardly arrived back in Harare when I received the bill - the request for support - with barely any documentation to justify such a large amount. It was as if the tour by itself was sufficient to get another chance at winning in the aid lottery.

These two caricatures - the Zimbabwean villagers in their traditional dress, poor yet beautiful, and the donor with deep pockets — bothered me so much that I came to distrust UN agencies even though I knew they were doing good work.

I could continue to list additional examples of interventions by development agencies in Zimbabwe, each of which would raise questions of ethics and very often of political sensibility. With hindsight, it appears as if I had been an actor in a great game of illusions which was easy to see through and yet was accepted by everyone.

At the heart of this hypocrisy are the principles and modi operandi of how development aid is implemented. We must take care to distinguish development aid from humanitarian aid, which is temporary and often vital.

What assumption is the necessity for this development aid based on? Why would Africa need this help more than other continents? There are two explanations for this, which are not mutually exclusive.

One of these concerns structural factors. The impoverishment of Africa can be explained by the effects of slavery and colonisation as well as the economic imbalances due to globalisation today, not to mention poor political governance.

The Cameroonian economist Célestin Monga refers to a 'tragic symphony of suffering', a sentiment constantly echoed by the 'good souls' of development aid. And yet one must admit that Africa cannot claim the monopoly on suffering or on enduring violence or on being economically dominated. Other regions of the world have received the same mistreatment, but they rely primarily on themselves to deal with it.

The other explanation is based on cultural differences. By this logic, impediments to development come from a recalcitrant cultural substrate, which explains to a large extent the apathetic and inconsistent attitude on the part of certain members of the African elite. This has been highlighted by the academic Axelle Kabou.

This may be partly true, but this approach furthers a type of essentialism which reduces people to biased clichés. And this approach is too quick to abandon the notion of personal and collective responsibility, which exists across all human cultures - including in Africa.

No matter how reasonable these approaches may be in reality, the worst part of them is that they consider Africa as an undifferentiated entity. Development operators - especially the UN agencies and the World Bank - have taken for granted that there is something special about Africa that is the same from the shores of Morocco down to the Cape of Good Hope, from the islands of Cabo Verde to the Somali coast.

Claude Lévi-Strauss already denounced the toxicity of this false evolutionism that considers all human societies to be part of the same developmental trajectory starting at a single origin and leading to a single endpoint. This economic and social Darwinism is locking the people of Africa into a history which is not their own.

This is exactly what I saw in Zimbabwe, where the donors fell into a rut, failing to adjust their intervention methods to the realities of the country.

The - mainly American - sanctions that the regime has been facing for many years are mostly responsible for making it impossible to access international financing. However, they have not kept Zimbabwe from receiving massive aid amounting to hundreds of millions of dollars of public Western funding, including from the US.

This money goes directly to the people by way of local or foreign charities, called 'civil society' charities. Not one penny passes through government entities.

Practically all of the UN agencies, the World Bank and the development operators - be they American (US-AID), British (DFID), German (GIZ), Swedish (SIDA), Dutch (FMO) or European (FED) - as well as many NGOs have taken charge of entire swaths of social life in Zimbabwe: health, education, access to water, women's rights, fighting AIDS and tuberculosis, child protection, etc.

The regime fully relies on these agencies to make up for its deficiencies; that way the national budget only has to cover the salaries of government employees.

De facto, the donors relieved the local authorities of some of their social responsibilities. Relieved in this way of its obligations, the regime can concentrate all its energy and means on securing its hold.

Not having contextualised their aid, the donors are now trapped. Morally, leaving the population to its fate is out of the question for the Westerners. Politically, however, this assistance reinforces the regime.

And, of course, the role of the UN representatives does not make it easier to resolve this problem.

The never-ceasing refrain of the UN - 'we must work with the governments in power' - gives Zimbabwe's regime a comfortable position. On the one hand, the regime enjoys the comprehensive machinery of the UN agencies. On the other hand, according to official propaganda, there is the evil West, which has still not come to terms with the country's independence.

An example, one amongst many, of this double dealing occurred in the spring of 2020, at the beginning of the covid crisis. At that time the local authorities asked the donors to pay for almost all the salaries of government medical staff (doctors and nurses).

Despite the tacit support of this request by the UN agencies, the Zimbabwe government had to acquiesce to the firm refusal from Western countries.

Two weeks later, the press reported on an inter-ministerial seminar which had taken place in a luxury hotel in Victoria Falls (300 dollars per night per person). The two main topics of this seminar were alcohol and prostitutes.

There is no need for me to expound on the utter cynicism of regimes which have completely failed since independence and yet feel free to accuse their former colonisers of being responsible for their failure. It is they who loudly demand rights and supplementary means from the West with no intent of giving them to their people.

At any rate, all my Western colleagues in Harare, and even some UN leaders, are aware of this fool's game. They just tolerate it, happy to help the population, at least. This is understandable.

The other hypocrisy is about how the EU works.

I saw with my own eyes the method with which the EU aims to multiply the creation of local organisations and NGOs which are all funded by public money from the EU. Thus, they create clients that perfectly fit the requirements - boxes to be ticked - created by the EU's central services.

Like the other development operators, the EU representatives 'create' their civil society, thus, in return, getting Brussels to validate their engagement and, of course, to validate the corresponding budgetary requests..

Actually, there is an ever-shifting landscape of civil organisations in Zimbabwe: the party in power, the military, the various oppositions, the various administrations, the tribal chiefs, the clans, the cities, the villages, the unions, the charities, the linguistic groups, etc.

Some groups work together, others oppose each other. But most have the same goal: to put themselves in the right place to profit from the revenue streams, whether they come from corruption, the parallel economy or Western aid.

Displaying only its role as an actor in development, the EU is seen in Harare like a type of large NGO - and definitely not like a political actor. I think it's about the same in all of Africa. The EU is locked into this posture, grudgingly playing a political role that keeps beckoning.

This European system of client creation is even more questionable from an institutional perspective. The EU finances as much as 75% of the budget of the SADC, an intergovernmental organisation that brings together 16 states in southern Africa and around the Indian Ocean.

The SADC is widely known for its political futility, professional incompetence and bureaucratic heaviness. The EU's objective is surely to tick the programme-related box 'assistance to regional organisations' without dealing with any follow-up monitoring.

Deep down, 'ticking boxes' may be the ultimate goal of the activities of the EU in Africa.

The lack of political action of the EU was very clear to me in Zimbabwe.

Every two weeks we had to suffer through soporific obligatory meetings with the European ambassadors and the EU representative where various questions were timidly touched upon but the possibilities of common initiatives were rarely brought up.

What's more, by request of the Spanish government with support from the Portuguese, it was now not allowed for active European ambassadors to publish common communiqués onsite. As far as emasculation goes, they could not have done any better!

Luckily, there were also informal donors' meetings - more precisely those of the active Western camp in Zimbabwe - which brought together the US, Canada, Australia, Japan, the UK, Germany, Sweden, the Netherlands, France and the EU representative.

These meetings weren't all at the highest level, but at least we spoke of politics, to the point of publishing common communiqués.

And we shared information that was often sensitive to coordinate the position we were taking.

It remains to be hoped that the geo-strategic situation of the moment will provoke a sea change in the EU, motivating it to change completely its ways of intervening in Africa.

The EU, backed by its member states, is Africa's number one business partner and number one investor. It is wrong for the EU to continue to let itself be perceived as if it were a simple NGO and a second-rate political player.

I had not planned to venture into these subjects with Tendaï. But one day, after a meeting at the EU representative's office which was even more draining than usual, I was weak enough to share my grief with him.

He did not reply, wilfully ignoring what I had said. This time he had brought along a young girl, about 12 years of age. He introduced her to me as Nyasha; she had been preceded by Chido, Tatenda, Missy, Blessing, Tanya and so many more, whose first names I have forgotten and who always shared in our meals in solemn silence.

They were all teenagers. They were always dressed modestly but had their own sense of proper attire: clean-shaven heads for the boys, neatly ironed clothes (down to their cloth skirts and trousers), proper closed shoes - and never flip-flops. This was in marked contrast to the appearance of the Rhodies, who, no matter their sex or age, would indulge in the pleasure of wearing wrinkled t-shirts, worn-out shorts and flip-flops and have disheveled hair.

I learned that the Rhodies liked to walk around like this - often even barefoot – to show everyone, and especially black people, that they were the owners of the country and would remain so. As if negligence in clothing were enough to challenge the new social order.

And so I met Nyasha, a young girl with a lively and intelligent expression. As with all of Tendaï's other guests, we first made some small talk before a long, awkward silence arose between us.

So I took up my tale of being a frustrated European official when Tendaï interrupted me.

'We'll talk about it once you have removed all your sanctions.'

Zimbabwe has been subject to sanctions by the West since the 2000s. To the authorities, the country's degraded economic situation was of American doing (European sanctions having no financial impact). Tendaï approved of this interpretation.

To the US, the main cause of the economic collapse is corruption, misgovernment and the lack of reforms.

In this game of chicken and egg, the elite 2% are not the ones suffering from the sanctions - they are easy for them to get around. Rather, it is the people who suffer. It is almost impossible for them to access a reliable currency and to live in a stable economy.

It's a complicated equation where ultimately the sanctions serve as a pretext for government propaganda to deny any responsibility for the economic and financial plight of the country.

Tendaï did not keep insisting on the question of sanctions. We both knew that it was a trap of a subject. He continued by denouncing development aid with a shocking argument.

'Look at how we live. Do you really think that all the money you have transferred for decades has helped us?!'

Full of sarcasm, he explained to me that any private company with a balance as mediocre as that of the professional 'helpers' would have declared bankruptcy long ago.

He went on, elaborating his central thesis that it was necessary for white people to go home and take their sanctions, their financial help, their aid programmes and all their so-called good will back with them.

Whilst he was speaking, he repeated many times, 'Don't come back till we give you a sign. We've got to get along without you first.'

Once again, Tendaï brought me to the limitations of my reasoning. And maybe he was correct. What gives us the right to think we have an 'obligation' to help African countries, and, what is more, doing a poor job at it and doing it only according to our criteria?

Even though it was available only in French at the time, I gave Tendaï the essay called 'Afrotopia' by the Senegalese writer and intellectual Felwine Sarr. He spoke to me about it for months. He copied whole pages onto Google Translate to understand the content of the book, which fascinated him, in English.

'This man from Senegal is right,' Tendaï would say. 'Let's think and act for ourselves!'

The best example of African players using modern tools to meet their needs for themselves can be found in the dizzying digital leap that Africa is engaged in.

Incredible creativity in mobile communications services in South Africa, Kenya and Nigeria, to name a few countries, is beyond dispute.

Skipping multiple technological steps, African entrepreneurs have captured this communication tool to create a method of payment and exchange so ingenious that it has been imported into some European countries.

In the most remote hinterlands of Zimbabwe, I have seen simple peasants perfectly master the services of this mobile-operated system with a degree of ease far surpassing the level of the general public in France.

In one of our soporific EU meetings, a European fellow diplomat of mine once remarked in a scandalised tone that this mobile tool was being used in Africa mostly for the unbridled consumption of pornography. I reminded everyone that this type of mobile phone use in Europe and the US generated revenues amounting to tens of billions of dollars. We Westerners thus had no lesson to give to Africa about the use of pornography. At least this one lively exchange made our meeting a little less boring.

With Tendaï I avoided this topic. His prim sense of modesty, very typical of Zimbabweans, led him to avoid such subjects.

In any event, he approved of my example of the success of mobile services in Africa, hastening to add that it was private companies that were driving this sector and not the government.

'That's always how it is for things that work in Africa,' he added. 'It comes from the private sector, and clearly the public sector doesn't like this. Look at our country. Econet, one of the best mobile phone operators in Africa, was invented by a Zimbabwean - and you know that this entrepreneur is banned from Zimbabwe!'

At this point in our conversation, I was very surprised that Tendaï would so directly question his Zanu comrades, not sheltering behind the inevitable 'it's someone else's fault' stance. I was soon reassured.

'It's well and good to give us the tools of your technologies, but we are still underneath a glass ceiling. You know as much as I do that most financial transactions between Africa and the rest of the world occur with you and the Chinese. It's a vertically dependent relationship which confines and suffocates us. Our governments have been trapped.

I couldn't let him get away with that.

'No, they trapped themselves. There is no international conspiracy against Africa. And, in my opinion, the more private sector initiatives there are, the greater will be your room to manoeuvre in Africa.

He shot a derisive smile at me.

'Yes, but we have to do this without you since your imperialism is incorrigible...'

No matter the basis on which future economic sovereignty of Africa will be built in the future, Tendaï and I agreed about one thing in today's reality: The donors must stop pretending that they are playing an essential role in their imaginary land of Africa, helping the equally imaginary African people.

CHAPTER V
COMING DEMOGRAPHIC UPHEAVALS

'There's only one man too many on earth and that is Thomas Malthus.'
Pierre-Joseph Proudhon
Philosophie de la misère
(published in English as: *The Philosophy of Misery*)

According to demographers themselves, demographic projections are just like weather predictions. They are quite reliable in the short term, extremely variable in the medium term and pure speculation over the long term.

A recent example illustrates the highly speculative nature of long-term demographic predictions. A study by HSBC - a bank whose ethical virtues we are familiar with - assures us that there will not be more than 4 billion people on earth in 2100, i.e. half as many as today (study available on the bank's website). The conclusion is that one should not worry about climate change and consequently not change any part of our economic model because demographic studies promise better days. Making demographic predictions say what we want them to is a rather common exercise in falsification.

This remains true if we refer to the demographic statistics available in sub-Saharan Africa to create projections on migration over a timeframe that is too far off.

Despite the good will of the experts of the UN and the World Bank, there aren't enough reliable data to make long-term assertions.

We have no exact census, no validated record of births and deaths, no reliable age pyramid, no precise snapshot of people's migrations, no documented profile of different classes, no effective border controls, etc.

This is true for southern Africa, as I could witness when I lived in Zimbabwe and as I travelled through Malawi.

Zimbabwe's surface area is about 400,000 km^2. That is three times the size of England and two-thirds that of mainland France. In this vast territory 13 to 15 million people are distributed in medium-sized cities and a vast countryside. The official data are wrong (17 million residents) and imprecise (1.5 to 2.5 million residents in Harare).

International observers carried out demographic crosschecks during the 2018 general elections. This allowed for a rough estimate of the population (about 15 million) as well as the number of city dwellers (a good third) and rural residents.

The population has been shrinking for the last 20 years due to continuous emigration. The elites and highly sought-after professionals (e.g. doctors and health professionals) go to the UK - Birmingham is a Zimbabwean city - Canada, Australia and the US. The less well-off go to South Africa.

This massive population drain even led to about 100 Zimbabweans relocating to The Falklands!

Whilst Zimbabwean immigration to the West is estimated to be over one million, immigration to South Africa amounts to two to four million workers, depending on the sources. That shows the scope of statistical discrepancy.

And yet Zimbabwe, which was considered the bread basket of Southern Africa, has the capacity to accommodate twice the current population.

The many reasons for this exodus include the collapse of agriculture, no network maintenance of the fresh water supply, increasing disappearance of public services, bouts of violence and political repression and the lack of attractive professional perspectives.

This is a true paradox: Zimbabwe is doubtlessly a country of emigration but also a country that takes in many immigrants, particularly from Malawi, a few hundred kilometres away. According to Malawi's ambassador in Harare, there are two to three million Malawians who live and work in Zimbabwe - yet another vey significant statistical discrepancy.

And that is understandable. Malawi is a true demographic bomb. Nearly 20 million residents are crammed onto 120,000 km² of which 30,000 are covered by a fresh water lake (Lake Malawi), which is largely polluted. There will be about 40 million people living in utter destitution 20 years from now.

Barely 8% of them have access to electricity (average in sub-Saharan Africa is about 50%). Most of them have had no choice but to destroy practically all their tropical forest for heating and cooking. Droughts are ever more formidable as is the irremediable erosion of the soil.

Some of Malawi's privileged classes - a very small number - are in the habit of dividing their time between the UK, the US and Malawi. But the large majority of Malawians tend to go Southwest (Zimbabwe and South Africa), joining the migration by underprivileged Zimbabweans toward their South African neighbour.

These migration waves are hard to quantify because there are practically no border controls beyond certain checkpoints on a very limited network of roads.

Of course, Malawian immigrants are not popular in Zimbabwe, and the same is true for Zimbabweans in South Africa. Racism and even racist attacks are unfortunately common. Sadly, there is nothing new under the sun.

I will avoid discussing South Africa as I do not understand the country well. I will just point out that it is the Eldorado for people from the surrounding area who are in difficulty - be they from Namibia, Botswana, Zimbabwe, Zambia, Malawi, Mozambique, Eswatini or Lesotho. This is due to its economic development, which is by no measure comparable to that of its neighbours. Its attractiveness extends all the way to the countries of the Congo basin.

Despite the vagueness of the available data, this rapid overview of the demographic situation in Zimbabwe and Malawi allows us to identify two distinct major movements:

• first, a numerically limited one toward rich countries (Europe, North America, Australia), for the wealthy and/or educated;

• second, a massive one toward the South African centre of economic development, for those who just want to live better.

When I mentioned this emigration to South Africa and the anti-immigrant climate to Tendaï, he launched into a long historical story to explain the violence, whether this be amongst South Africans or directed at immigrants.

He explained to me that the origin of all this violence lay in the Dutch and British colonisations which were marked by extreme brutality, and made worse by wars amongst the white people - Boers against British - which, according to Tendaï, led to the deaths of hundreds of thousands of black people involved in these events.

Then there was the great Zulu king Shaka Zulu, whose military expansionism led to the 'dispersal' of the black population of the region (known as *mfecane* in the Zulu language). Shaka's conquests displaced a large number of peoples and caused a split in the Zulu tribes. This explains how the Ndebeles arrived in southern Zimbabwe. And then there was the ruthless and cruel domination by the white people during apartheid.

'Three hundred years of continuous violence - murderous wars and interracial settling of scores! So much blood, so much hatred and so much rancour, all accumulated! And that is not all,' Tendaï continued.

He repeated his conviction that Nelson Mandela was wrong to believe in a rainbow society. The evil is anchored too deeply for the well-intentioned to overcome it. It cannot be removed.

I remarked that in reality, racism amongst black people and between black people and mixed-race people is just as virulent as racism between white people and black people. He shrugged his shoulders before answering.

'White people don't have a monopoly on hatred.'

To him, civil society in South Africa was built on violence - often deadly violence. Thus, it only knew this mode of relating to itself or to others to solve its problems. He took on a prophetic air.

'The worst is yet to come for us in South Africa.'

I was most surprised by his reaction to my reflections on the exodus of a part of the Zimbabwean elites to the West. Hearing me talk about the large-scale arrival of Africans in Europe filled him with joy.

'It's your turn to see what it does to you to be invaded by foreigners of a different skin colour. To each his turn!'

He was shaken by a full-throated laugh.

'To each his turn,' he repeated several times.

All the arguments I brought up were to no avail: the difficulties of integration in Europe, increasing racism, the need not to rob African countries of their most competent people, the dangers of un-documented immigration. To Tendaï, this was a fair reversal of the situation. Europeans now had to pay the price for what they had inflicted on African people.

His remark brought to mind the title of a book by Portuguese writer Antonio Lobo Antunes, called *The Return of the Caravels*. Tendaï wanted these caravels not to be laden with the riches stolen by white people but to be full of formerly oppressed people coming to take their revenge.

I couldn't leave it at that, so I decided to educate myself more, not only to satisfy my curiosity but also to support my discussion with Tendaï.

The first thing I learned was that it makes no sense to consider the peoples of Africa as a single demographic entity powered by a single dynamic.

Scholars distinguish five distinct territories in sub-Saharan Africa: the Sahel, the Gulf of Guinea, Central Africa, Eastern Africa and Southern Africa. In each of these areas there are different demographic dynamics, at least according to the approximate estimations that have been made to date. And then, inside of each of these regions, we must be aware that there are nuances, some of which may be decisive.

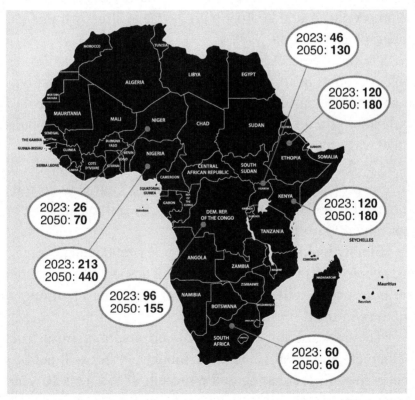

The demographic projections done for sub-Saharan Africa, as established by the UN, are impressive, even if they are only approximations.

In the next generation, i.e. around the year 2050, there will be a population of 270 million in the Sahel, 70 million of which will be located in Niger; 600 million in the Gulf of Guinea region, of which 440 will be in Nigeria; 270 million in Central Africa, of which 155 will be in the Democratic Republic of Congo; 690 million in Eastern Africa, of which 180 million will be in Ethiopia, and finally, 330 million in Southern Africa, of which 60 million will be in South Africa.

We should note that just like Northern Africa (the sixth demographic territory in Africa which is projected to have 290 million people around 2050), South Africa is already undergoing a demographic transition.

On the whole, Africa is projected to be home to 2.5 billion people, amounting to one fourth of the human poplulation. For comparison, the current population there is 1.3 billion people. The population in the 1930s was around 150 million and the population in 1650 was around 100 million.

On the other hand, we see that in 2050, the population of France is projected to be 72 million, that of Germany 76 million, that of the EU 450 million, that of the UK 79 million and that of the US around 400 million.

Simply looking at these figures, one would tend to agree with those people who predict that the African demographic abundance, seen as a whole, will necessarily lead to waves of immigration from the continent - primarily to Europe.

They take it for granted that job creation, infrastructure development and improvements in public services will not be able to keep up with the demographic growth of the next 20 years in sub-Saharan Africa.

But what is really going to happen? Will the massive emigration to Europe of African populations in search of a better future really take place?

Nothing about this is certain.

If we, like the scientists, focus on the five areas of population that constitute Africa's demographic landscape, we get a more nuanced understanding of the matter; it is less sensationalist and, above all, better matches the different realities of the different Africas.

The experts broadly distinguish three areas where economic development is real, even if it is chaotic and unequal. They are: Western Africa around Ivory Coast, Nigeria and Ghana; Eastern Africa with Ethiopia and Kenya and, finally, Southern Africa with South Africa. We should note that these three drivers of economic growth are located on the coasts.

The Sahel, the fourth demographic area, covers nine countries from Mauritania to Eritrea. This vast area will experience great cumulative difficulties with no identifiable field of development in sight: decreasing agricultural yields, accelerated urbanisation, dependence on international aid, and the increasing impact of climate change.

Finally, Central Africa, the fifth demographic area, extending from Sudan to Namibia in an area across the Congo basin, is said to have a low population density (an 'empty diagonal', as French demographers would call this). Kinshasa is the noteworthy exception. It is expected to reach a population of 35 million residents by 2050.

We don't have to be great experts to discern three distinct migratory movements:

- first, a powerful movement from the interior of the continent where millions of poor people living in landlocked areas will head to the coastal centres of economic development mentioned above;
- second, a significantly smaller movement by the elites and upper middle classes toward Europe, North America and Australia;
- third, a numerically smaller movement where desperate people will do all they can to reach the coasts of Europe. This migration will only involve a few thousand people per year according to the UN International Organisation of Migration (IOM) since European border control has intensified and the knowledge of the dangers of this journey has increased, especially in the Sahel.

Some numerical data exist about migratory movements within Africa, and these confirm this powerful migration from underprivileged areas to the coastal regions where development is taking place. According to the World Bank, in 2019, about 80% of African migrants moved from the continent's interior toward North Africa, the Gulf of Guinea, Eastern Africa and Southern Africa.

When it comes to the emigration from the continent of the privileged and educated classes, the World Bank estimates that 2% of the population have a disposable income over 20 dollars per day and almost 6% have a disposable income of between 10 and 20 dollars per day.

So, about 8% of the population have over ten dollars per day and can be considered part of this so-called privileged class.

Let us suppose that one third - which is a high estimate - of these people with an income of over 10 dollars per day decide to move to the rich countries. By 2050, that would be equal to 2 to 3% of the 2.5 billion estimated African residents, amounting to 50 to 75 million people.

The World Bank notes that currently amongst this so-called privileged class of the African population, half emigrate to Europe and the other half to the rest of the world (mainly Australia and North America).

Based on this distribution, in 2050, we can expect the arrival of these people in Europe in large numbers - 25 to 40 million. This is a far cry from the doom-saying projections we see here and there. The European Commission uses the lower of these estimates (about 25 million) to state a number for the Africans who will move to the European Union by 2050.

Armed with my figures and supporting documents, I explained to Tendaï what the scenarios of the coming demographic explosion were likely to be.

He conscientiously took in all the information I gave him, taking the time to ask for clarification on points he found too vague. He was so passionate about the subject that our lunch lasted late into the afternoon. I also knew he would check all available statistics on the web.

He summed up our conversation perfectly -

'Some of the competent people are running away to Europe, America and Australia, whilst massive numbers of the others are emigrating to South Africa. What's happening in Zimbabwe now will be repeated on a large scale in all of Africa.'

Whilst one could indeed fear a sort of human tsunami, it would be unlikely to spread beyond Africa but rather move from the underprivileged hinterlands toward the prosperous areas on the coasts.

If such a population shift were to take place, one could indeed also fear human tragedies and issues with security, coupled with various forms of local destabilisation.

Today, European countries are content with an understanding that is too general — the pressure of African migration is seen without nuances. This leads them to be wrong. If there is indeed a threat, it is mostly directed at a definite number of African coastal nations.

What one must fear is that Europe, intoxicated by its partial analyses, will only bet on the benefits of reinforcing its southern borders on the Mediterranean and, thus, will run the risk of finding itself locked into a fortress of senior citizens by 2050 (over one third of the European population will be over 60). This fortress will be surrounded by young Asians (47% of the world population aged 0-24) and young Africans (37% of the world population aged 0-24) who are propelled by their formidable energy.

Authors and analysts who work on these demographic questions are right to alert public opinion to these demographic movements in Africa.

They do so emphatically even if some of them would benefit from using finer brushes to paint their portrait of human geography in sub-Saharan Africa rather than wielding an analytic trowel.

It would be more important still for the African elites to address the subject more forcefully - some already do - to push their governments into action.

But some of the globalised African elites already have their seats reserved at European and American tables. And in this matter it's easier to theorise about Africanist concepts off-site than to inconvenience one's hosts by bringing up crucial problems that don't have an obvious solution.

The African intellectual class - especially amongst the elites of the diaspora - has been dealing with these questions of demographics with a disastrous analytic blindness.

CHAPTER VI

THE RAVAGES OF CORRUPTION

'A type of small caste with long teeth, greedy and insatiable...'

Frantz Fanon

Les damnés de la terre

(published in English as: *The Wretched of the Earth*)

The German NGO Transparency International publishes an annual Corruption Perceptions Index (CPI) on 180 countries.

Of the 50 countries at the bottom of the list, 25 are in Africa and 12 of these are in the group of the 20 most corrupt countries.

Of the 50 countries seen as the least corrupt, four are located in sub-Saharan Africa: Seychelles, Cabo Verde, Botswana and Mauritius. Yes, these countries have small populations and are islands, archipelagos or - in the case of Botswana - a desert land. But they are proof that there is nothing distinctly African about corruption.

CORRUPTION PERCEPTIONS INDEX 2022

The perceived levels of public sector corruption in 180 countries/territories around the world.

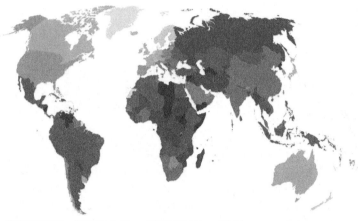

SCORE COUNTRY/TERRITORY

Score	Country	Score	Country	Score	Country	Score	Country	Score	Country	Score	Country	Score	Country
90	Denmark	67	Chile	52	Grenada	42	Solomon Islands	36	Sri Lanka	30	Mauritania	23	Iraq
87	Finland	67	United Arab Emirates	51	Malta	42	Timor-Leste	36	Thailand	30	Papua New Guinea	23	Myanmar
87	New Zealand	65	Barbados	51	Rwanda	42	Trinidad and Tobago	36	Turkey	30	Togo	23	Zimbabwe
84	Norway	64	Bahamas	51	Saudi Arabia	42	Vietnam	34	Bosnia and Herzegovina	29	Gabon	22	Eritrea
83	Singapore	63	Israel	50	Croatia	41	Kosovo	34	Gambia	28	Mali	22	Sudan
83	Sweden	63	Korea, South	50	Mauritius	40	Guyana	34	Indonesia	28	Paraguay	21	Congo
82	Switzerland	62	Lithuania	49	Namibia	40	India	34	Malawi	28	Russia	21	Guinea Bissau
80	Netherlands	62	Portugal	48	Vanuatu	40	Maldives	34	Nepal	27	Kyrgyzstan	20	Democratic Republic of the Congo
79	Germany	60	Botswana	47	Jordan	40	North Macedonia	33	Sierra Leone	27	Pakistan	19	Chad
77	Ireland	60	Cabo Verde	46	Armenia	40	Suriname	33	Algeria	26	Cameroon	19	Comoros
77	Luxembourg	60	Saint Vincent and the Grenadines	46	Romania	40	Tunisia	33	Angola	26	Liberia	19	Nicaragua
76	Hong Kong	66	Spain	45	China	39	Belarus	33	El Salvador	26	Madagascar	19	Turkmenistan
75	Australia	56	Latvia	45	Cuba	39	Colombia	33	Mongolia	26	Mozambique	18	Burundi
74	Canada	58	Qatar	45	Montenegro	39	Moldova	33	Philippines	26	Uganda	17	Equatorial Guinea
74	Estonia	57	Czechia	45	Sao Tome and Principe	38	Argentina	33	Ukraine	25	Bangladesh	17	Haiti
74	Iceland	56	Georgia	44	Bahrain	38	Brazil	33	Zambia	25	Guinea	17	Korea, North
74	Uruguay	56	Italy	44	Jamaica	38	Ethiopia	32	Dominican Republic	25	Iran	17	Libya
73	Belgium	56	Slovenia	44	Oman	38	Morocco	32	Kenya	24	Afghanistan	16	Yemen
73	Japan	55	Dominica	43	Benin	38	Tanzania	32	Niger	24	Cambodia	14	Venezuela
73	United Kingdom	55	Poland	43	Bulgaria	38	Cote d'Ivoire	31	Bolivia	24	Central African Republic	13	South Sudan
72	France	55	Saint Lucia	43	Ghana	37	Lesotho	31	Laos	24	Guatemala	13	Syria
71	Austria	53	Costa Rica	43	Senegal	36	Albania	31	Mexico	24	Lebanon	12	Somalia
70	Seychelles	53	Fiji	43	South Africa	36	Ecuador	31	Uzbekistan	24	Nigeria		
69	United States of America	52	Slovakia	42	Burkina Faso	36	Kazakhstan	30	Djibouti	24	Tajikistan		
68	Bhutan	52	Cyprus	42	Hungary	36	Panama	30	Egypt	23	Azerbaijan		
68	Taiwan	52	Greece	42	Kuwait	36	Peru	30	Eswatini	23	Honduras		
						36	Serbia						

SCORE

Highly Corrupt ... Very Clean

0-9 · 10-19 · 20-29 · 30-39 · 40-49 · 50-59 · 60-69 · 70-79 · 80-89 · 90-100 · No Data · Disputed Boundaries* · Lines of Combat*

#cpi2022
www.transparency.org/cpi

The rank of a country in the CPI Top 50 charts is certainly important, but the criteria published by this NGO are just as interesting. They allow us to measure the dynamics at play in the fight against corruption that some countries wage.

Here we take note that, since 2012, 23 countries have had their rankings lowered - including such luminaries as Australia, Canada, the United States and Luxembourg.

At the same time, several countries have significantly moved up on the chart. Amongst these are Angola, Ivory Coast, Senegal, Tanzania and - we must add - South Africa.

Unfortunately for the citizens of Zimbabwe, their country is not rated amongst the best in the CPI ranking.

The issue of corruption disturbed Tendaï, who could not accept that his comrades from the heroic times had renounced their ideals in the greedy pursuit of ill-gotten wealth. He was convinced that a promising political solution in Zimbabwe could only be envisioned if the members and friends of the Zanu would stop considering their country as if it were their private property.

To him, the Zanu with its 'nebula' (the military and security forces) were stuck with practices they had inherited from the white people of Rhodesia, the Rhodies.

To Tendaï, his former comrades were walking in the footsteps of their predecessors by seizing all the economic power to the detriment of the people. I now understood why Zimbabweans colloquially called anyone who was associated with power after independence - whether closely or loosely - 'black Rhodies'.

It is a terrible irony of history that liberators take on the oppressive practices of their former masters, substituting endemic corruption for systematic dispossession.

When Tendaï illustrated his point by telling me the incredible story of the diamonds of Marange, I had my doubts. I was not receptive to the rumours and other exaggerations that Zimbabweans generally like to view as absolute truths. I was wrong.

That day Tendaï had insisted that we have lunch right in the centre of Harare, in a type of small, working-class self-service restaurant, which was located on the ground floor of a concrete building, the Eastgate Building. Like many cities that follow a British urban blueprint, Harare is spread out around large green spaces in the form of parks and squares where the streets divide up residential areas that are carefully separated from each other and classified according to the social class of their residents.

The buildings rarely have more than two storeys except in the city centre, where colonial-era buildings, usually poorly maintained, rub shoulders with modern buildings of the worst architectural taste. This landscape extends southwestward in an immense working-class neighbourhood that resembles a pre-liberation South African 'township' and is called Mbare. Here, a very large number of people is crammed together and left to its own devices to survive. Despite its relative aesthetic chaos, Mbare teems with life in a way that is much more captivating and much more joyful than that of the rest of the city, where people are thoroughly bored. Like most provincial British capitals, Harare is a sad city.

Tendaï knew of my reservations about his city, so he wanted me to see the Eastgate Building, erected in the late 1990s upon the request of Robert Mugabe. This building is an ecosystem unto itself. Tendaï called it 'a living machine'.

And indeed, the Zimbabwean architect was inspired by the ventilation system of termite mounds when he designed this impressive seven-storey building. There is no need for air-conditioning; instead, the air circulates in a clever natural flow.

Eastgate Building and an ant hill for comparison

Tendaï was very proud of it. There was no point in calling his attention to the fact that the building evidently had not seen much maintenance since the 1990s, as indicated by the broken window panes, corroded concrete, rusted metal reinforcements, abandoned shops, etc. It looked just like all other infrastructure projects from that period in the country, which, without exception, had been neglected or completely abandoned.

Harare is a capital adrift, whose old-fashioned appeal cannot hide its dilapidation. The Eastgate Building is the perfect example of this. I felt obliged to share in Tendaï's satisfaction in the detailed description he gave of the building we were dining in.

'Just see what we are capable of building,' he said. 'But we have the curse of gold and diamonds.'

That's when he told me the incredible story of the diamonds of Marange.

Near the village of Marange, in eastern Zimbabwe, only a stone's throw from the border with Mozambique, there was one of the greatest concentrations of diamonds in the world in an area of about 600 km²! Late in 2006, these often easily accessible diamonds gave rise to a veritable diamond rush. For several months, almost 50,000 people from all across the country eagerly engaged in picking up and selling rough diamonds. It was common to see young people along the roads who sold plastic buckets full of these rough precious stones for nothing more than a 100 dollars — even in the city of Harare. Thus, small fortunes were made in a very short time.

But soon the army and security forces brutally put an end to this wild exploitation by taking full control of the diamond extraction.

Licenses were given to Zimbabwean state-owned enterprises, which were connected to Chinese and Lebanese entities. They plundered the site for profit and played an active role in the fraudulent enrichment of the military (of all ranks), the security forces and the pillars of the regime.

The authorities officially announced an income of about 1.5 billion dollars per year starting in 2010, when the large-scale operation started. In 2016, one could thus expect an income of about 9 billion dollars.

That's when the scandal exploded. Almost none of the money ever arrived in government coffers. In the summer of 2016, Robert Mugabe himself publicly expressed his surprise about the 'disappearance' of the revenue from diamond mining. This made front page news.

Tendaï saw this as evidence that his hero was surrounded by the wrong people. I refrained from commenting on Bob's obscene cynicism. The story of the diamonds of Marange ended in 2017. Due to the lack of significant investment in equipment, diamond extraction came to a near complete standstill.

To get a better idea of the negligence of the people who shamelessly profited from selling the diamonds, it may help to compare these evaporated 9 billion dollars with three basic data points: in 2016, Zimbabwe's external public debt was a little over 8 billion dollars, its gross domestic product was about 22 billion dollars and the government budget was about 4 billion dollars (just for the salary of government employees).

That means the revenue from the diamonds would have been enough for Zimbabwe to restore its public finances, reduce its external public debt and massively invest in education, health, and infrastructure.

I mentioned to Tendaï that corruption was equally flourishing in the four main mining industries of Zimbabwe: gold, platinum, chromium and nickel, not to mention rare earths, for which no data are available.

For gold alone, the official declared production was about 25 tonnes per year on average. According to experts from the IMF, the true figure reached somewhere between 35 and 40 tonnes per year. That makes for 10 to 15 tonnes that are under the radar.

The most striking thing of all is that this traffic in gold keeps happening in plain view. A network of small gold miners is controlled by the higher-ups of the hierarchy or even the president himself. It operates the many gold mines the country is blessed with. With utter impunity, tonnes of gold secretly leave Zimbabwe, depriving the population of a good that belongs to it. For years now, social media have been buzzing with overwhelming evidence against traffickers - to no avail. Even TV station Al Jazeera's well-documented report from 2023 is not about to change the predatory behaviour around gold.

When you are a diplomat, it's not uncommon in Harare for a member of the nomenklatura to ask you to send abroad dozens or hundreds of kilos of gold under diplomatic cover. I can vouch for this since it was suggested to me without any embarrassment as a simple favour amongst friends. Nothing is beyond the pale for the gold traffickers, who are all connected to the regime. There are no constraints, least of all the constraint that the best interests of the people of Zimbabwe should be taken into account.

This phenomenon of massive corruption is an open secret.

In 2019, the American ambassador was being interviewed on public television during prime time. He brought up the dozens of billions of dollars that had been misused in the preceding 20 years.

The Zimbabwean journalist sitting across from him almost fainted at the idea that the diplomat could give the names of the beneficiaries, the channels used or even the bank account numbers that had been identified abroad.

Once again, Tendaï surprised me. This information did not phase him. As usual, he connected it to the legacy of colonialism.

In 1969, Rhodesia had passed a series of laws imposing conditions on extractive mining operations in the country (called the Mines and Minerals Act). These laws stipulated that the president was considered to be the owner of the country's mineral resources. In spite of the many amendments which had been made to these texts since independence, that part - the privatisation of the mining resources solely to benefit the president - had never been repealed.

'You see, we preserved two things right from the Rhodies with no changes at all: this absurd law and the CIO!' he exclaimed with a hearty laugh.

The CIO (Central Intelligence Organisation) was Rhodesia's feared and efficient secret service agency. Zimbabwe retained its culture, its practices and even its name. The CIO was and continues to be the discreet and powerful armed branch of the regime exerting its authoritarian control of the country.

Tendaï saw another explication for this systemic corruption. And that was the presence of China, which he perceived as the new face of the coloniser.

It is true that, using a well established approach, Beijing had offered its services to Zimbabwe for its infrastructure projects (airport, roads, bridges, parliament, stadium, railroads, etc), sometimes for free, in exchange for priority access to the country's minerals, a source of all kinds of compromising behaviours.

Like all observers, Tendaï had noted that China only used Chinese workers on its construction sites and also in the mining operations it had been granted. Such activities were always carried out by Chinese companies with Chinese financing. The more China was in control of all parts of the process from beginning to end, the more it served its own interests.

The resulting tension with the local people, who benefited only marginally from the few new jobs, strengthened the latent anti-Chinese racism which manifested itself blatantly once the coronavirus began to spread in March 2020. The Chinese presence in Zimbabwe, which had amounted to tens of thousands of people, evaporated from one day to the next.

Beyond the hidden hostility from the Zimbabweans, Chinese companies were confronted with new mechanisms of dependence caused by a corruption whose existence they never suspected, despite being masters in the field themselves. I had the chance to give Tendaï an example of this. Tendaï was overjoyed.

China had obtained the concessions for two mining sites where they had expected to find gold. Having invested nearly 300 million dollars - mining operations always require a massive initial investment - the Chinese company discovered significant gold deposits. Acting against all their obligations, the authorities of Zimbabwe nationalised both mines right away, provoking anger from the Chinese. To calm their partners, Zimbabwe granted two new concessions, probably for rare earth elements.

I got this information right from the Chinese ambassador at the time, who did not hide his desire to leave Zimbabwe.

So, the more China became financially involved in the country, the more it fell under the influence of the masters of corruption and bad faith, making it increasingly hard to pull out without paying a very high price for it.

The most absurd part of this story is that, once the gold which was close to the surface had been exploited, the two mines had to be abandoned since upkeep and replacement of the mining equipment was not included in the plans of the 'nationalisers'.

I could also have mentioned to Tendaï the renovation of Harare's international airport by the Chinese. It was almost completed in 2019, but the project stayed unfinished for months due to the absence of 10 million dollars which had disappeared into the pockets of Zimbabwe officials.

The experts are correct to point out that China is inexorably moving its pawns forward in sub-Saharan Africa. 1.1 million Chinese people and 10,000 companies are already there, generating transactions of more than 200 billion dollars. Their positioning in the strategic sector of digital technology is becoming ever more aggressive.

However, my experience in Zimbabwe leads me to view their chances of building a stable, long-term partnership somewhat skeptically. Looking at things in perspective, it seems that 'Chinafrica' is beginning more and more to resemble 'Francafrica'. The same naiveté and mistakes are leading to the same results — the accumulation of irredeemable debts, which amplifies economic disillusionment and political frustration, bringing to the fore an ever less concealed rejection in the end.

The true story of China in Africa still remains to be written.

No matter how much I explained to Tendaï that by

discouraging investors - even Chinese investors - his country would cut off the financial means it needed to exploit its immense mineral resources, he would not budge.

'So much the better. These natural resources are a curse!' he would reply each time the subject came up.

He wasn't the only one to say that all the money too easily obtained from the mining concessions had twisted the minds of the leaders and turned a large part of the country's active population into rentiers who were obsessed with grabbing their share of the pie.

But Tendaï always ended up accusing others of being responsible for this.

'And why has all of this happened? So that Zurich, Singapore and Shanghai could become the wealthiest cities of Africa! Thank you, dear West, and thank you, dear China!'

This indisputable aspect of reality could not conceal another aspect, however, which is that these financial transfers away from Africa could not have taken place if the governments and some of the elites had not been interested parties - not to say accomplices.

Whilst I recognised that Tendaï was partly right, I was still tired of hearing the same old tune, 'others are to blame', every time we talked about a serious problem in Zimbabwe.

And so it came about that one day in October 2017 I had the chance to get back at Tendaï.

We were meeting at the little veranda of a Greek snack-bar in the Kensington neighbourhood. I had arrived a bit early and I could see Tendaï approaching on foot. With his slow step, holding his head high and looking around, he cut a fine figure. The angles of his gaunt face were highlighted by his cropped curly hair. Tendaï was clutching his customary little black briefcase made of synthetic leather, making him look like a retired primary school teacher.

For the first time I saw how thin he was. He looked as if he were floating in his old faded white safari jacket with his cream-coloured canvas trousers concealing the movement of his legs.

In Harare, a person's body weight was generally a reliable indicator of his or her social class. The more extra body fat the person carried, the higher the likelihood that the person belonged to the privileged class. This was particularly true of women who had close connections to power. To them being corpulent or obese was a matter of honour. Unless he had a peculiar metabolism, Tendaï was apparently not a member of the 'well-fed' class.

In fact, despite all my attempts, I knew nothing about him — not where he lived, not where he was from originally and even less his career path as a veteran of the revolution. Each time I tried to broach any of these topics, he changed the subject. And not once did he ask me a question about my personal life.

I played along with it. Our relationship was purely an intellectual one - spiced up with the flavour of the overly salty dishes served in Harare's supermarket snack-bars.

I was going to get back to the subject of corruption when the police set up a road-block in the street only a few metres away from us on the pretext of carrying out vehicle inspections, but with the true motive of extorting money from the drivers.

We observed the money dance as the bills changed hands - one, five, or ten dollars - from the drivers to the police. Those who escaped this 'tax' wore signs of belonging to the party or benefited from their status as part of the government apparatus. Apart from these exceptions, there was no escape. Everyone had to pay — even the drivers of the 'commuters', private minibuses that crisscrossed the country since public transport was lacking in Zimbabwe.

I knew some of the racketeered money would end up in the pockets of the individual officers. But it also allowed the Zimbabwe police to pay for equipment (vehicles and uniforms) because the government didn't spend as much as one dollar on ensuring its institutions functioned, and even less on investing in their modernisation. Each public sector got by as best it could.

Looking at this spectacle, I had an opportunity to tease Tendaï a bit. I remarked, 'Look, the Westerners and the Chinese have nothing to do with this!'

Tendaï took some time before he responded to my little provocation.

'My country is in bad shape, in very bad shape.'

He basically explained to me that in Zimbabwe corruption was a type of transaction that had become common amongst his fellow citizens. It had started after independence at the very top of the social ladder. Year after year it had spread from the ruling classes to the bottom rung of society. It now reached ordinary citizens, even the poorest of them.

'Zimbabweans are not corrupt by nature,' he proclaimed. 'It is that the system of general corruption has taken deep roots.'

He knew that corruption would have deleterious effects in the long run, rotting all levels of society to the core with its unwritten rules and its logic.

Watching Tendaï's face tense up, I understood that this painful reality made him suffer.

I could have told him that the economic theory of trickle down (when the richer get richer the less monied classes can benefit from this because the money trickles down to them) turned out to be an illusion in countries with well structured economies, but, in contrast, it worked pretty well when it came to trickling down corruption.

I refrained from offering any such commentary.

It was intolerable to him to see this unhealthy mode of interpersonal relationships take hold of his country. He knew that for many of his fellow citizens the need to survive brought them to compromise themselves in the hope of being able to benefit, when it was their turn, from such transactions and the game of converting influence into money. The virus had spread and massively infected the population.

And yet, amidst this society where mistrust, informing on people, and lies undermined social solidarity, some Zimbabweans, both black and white, refused to engage in these destructive behaviours. Tendaï was one of them. It was a matter of pride to him.

The opacity of these corruptive practices would make it difficult to attach any serious numbers to this phenomenon. Nevertheless, the degree of importance of the informal sector in the economic and social lives of the 15 million residents would serve as an indirect indicator that could help measure the concentration of wealth.

According to official statistics from Zimstat in 2016, six million people worked in the informal sector. That is 95% of the working population, whilst the formal economy employed only 400,000 people!

So it was thanks to a sort of parallel world that the great majority of the population was able to survive. Of course, this economic structure would be fragile, often transitory and would lend itself to all types of unofficial economic activity. Not being financed by banks, this parallel world has a weak structure and does not benefit from any government assistance.

Worse, the authorities take advantage of the situation to exempt themselves from any policies encouraging stable job creation. After all, the informal economy serves to absorb the recurring insufficiencies of the labour market.

A privileged caste in control of mining resources, a small, rickety formal sector, and a vast informal sector left to itself, this three-speed society is not particular to Zimbabwe.

A major example of such a society is the case of the Democratic Republic of Congo. The DRC was the subject of multiple reports by UN experts which were based on very precise and documented data. They denounced the fraudulent practices of the worldwide mining conglomerates which ravaged the country. This changed almost nothing.

NGOs also called attention to the ambivalent attitude of Canada, home to the largest market for products of mineral extraction in Toronto (amounting to 50% of world trade) without taking into consideration the conditions under which the minerals were extracted. Once again, there was no change.

So, business continued as usual, providing Tendaï and many other Zimbabweans with grist for the mill. They got information online and were not fooled by the double speak of certain Western players.

The same was true for the American ambassador's televised remarks about the astronomical sums that had been embezzled in Zimbabwe over the last twenty years. Tendaï could not understand why the US didn't publish the names of all the fraudulent parties and the exact amounts they stole as well as the list of complicit banks.

To him, the Americans kept this information private because they derived a financial benefit from the tax havens which they protected. In Harare, as in all parts of the world, belief in conspiracies unfortunately is never very far away.

To Tendaï the most shocking part of it was that white people had concluded that all Africans, and thus all of Africa, were predisposed to being dishonest and evasive after they themselves had profited from several obvious cases of corruption in this or that African country, such as Zimbabwe.

The information from the NGO Transparency International that I gave him strengthened his interpretation that it made no sense to put all African countries into the same basket.

Tendaï's argument was that if the same logic were applied to Europe, it would lead to the conclusion that Europeans as a whole are all corrupt since Luxembourg, Monaco, the Netherlands, the City of London and Switzerland are regularly singled out for money laundering, mountains of fiscal optimisations and refusing to pay taxes.

The same goes for the US. Delaware has been a famous tax haven for decades. In other words, it's been the benchmark for the darkest financial machinations. I might add that the current US President was a Delaware senator from 1973 to 2009.

Do we conclude that Joe Biden is corrupt and the entire US is a land of corruption? Of course not.

'It's a double standard when you compare it to the lot given to the African countries,' Tendai added.

I had to admit that he wasn't entirely wrong about this. If we consider the amounts at stake, this double standard is even more flagrant. To take the example of France, every year the amount of fiscal fraud - and it really is fraudulent practice since it amounts to embezzlement - is estimated by the ministry of finance to be around 100 billion euros. With these statistics, France would be considered one of the most corrupt countries if it were in Africa.

Let's now consider the total amount of monies in the US and in Europe that are stolen, laundered, or which are fraudulently withheld. The conclusion is obvious. The amount of money embezzled and the sophistication of the corruption would leave Africa in the dust. The West is a lot more efficient!

Like all other countries in the world, without exception, African countries experience the evil of corruption. Unfortunately for Tendaï, Zimbabwe's case is one of the most distressing as far as systemic corruption is concerned. He felt it in his very being.

On the day we saw the road-block, I noticed his exhaustion and I wanted to lighten his spirits by telling him the joke of the scorpion that wanted to cross a river on the back of a buffalo. To this day I don't know why the idea crossed my mind. Perhaps I was inspired by the fatalistic attitude of the drivers who were being fleeced before our eyes.

The buffalo at first refused to carry the scorpion, fearing that it would get stung. To this the scorpion replied, 'I won't sting you because you would drown, and so would I.' In the middle of the river, the scorpion couldn't refrain from stinging the buffalo. The shocked buffalo asked, 'Why did you do it?' The scorpion replied, 'That's Africa for you.'

It would have been better if I hadn't told the story.

For the first time, Tendaï raised his voice so much that that other guests at the tables around us were startled by the altercation.

He accused me of being just like other white people who considered black people to be inconsistent and suicidal and of seeing Africa as nothing more than a vague group of genetically corrupt humans.

No matter how much I insisted that there was nothing insidious behind my bad joke, he would not calm down.

Evidently there is no inevitable link between black people and the plague of corruption. Evidently some African nations fought as hard as they could to stem this curse. And evidently there is a tendency in the West to put Africa and corruption in the same basket too easily. Evidently... He was no longer listening to me. He continued shouting as he was leaving the snack-bar.

I was convinced that I wouldn't see Tendaï again, and I was down on myself for having brought up the topic of corruption, a subject which pained him so much, in such a maladroit, joking tone.

Five days later I received a package addressed to me at the embassy. It was a block of amber with a small black scorpion trapped inside. It was accompanied by a note, which Tendaï had gone to the trouble of writing in French: 'Il ne piquera plus personne' (it won't sting anyone anymore).

This elegant gesture was typical of the concern for self-control and courtesy that is so common amongst people from

Zimbabwe. One mustn't raise one's voice even if one doesn't agree. Getting carried away is a sign of weakness reserved for white people, as I often heard people say. Receiving this gift made me feel even more embarrassed. After all, it was up to me to apologise to him.

At our next meeting, I presented him with a copy of a small sculpture by the famous Zimbabwean artist Henry Munyaradzi, who died in 1998. It was the sculptor's rendition of Rodin's *The Thinker*. I included a note which said in English 'Think before you speak.'

CHAPTER VII

BY WAY OF CONCLUSION

'What is to be done?'
Lenin

In the preceding chapters I hope I have been able to illustrate in a concrete manner a certain number of characteristics of Zimbabwe: the negligence of a regime that is obsessed with maintaining its privileges, the importance of being grounded in the culture and the history of the country, the necessary calling into question of the logic of the professional helpers, the imperative need for supporting local entrepreneurs, especially in the digital sector, a realistic look at demographic trends and, finally, the cancer that is systematised corruption.

What is true for Zimbabwe can be extended to other African countries. Many observers - journalists, experts, and diplomats - both Africans and Westerners, have already identified these problem areas.

So, what is to be done?

I will take the risk of proposing three areas of intervention whose relevance in the field I was able to assess directly: Africa to the Africans; the actions of France and the European Union; and the unity of Zimbabwe.

AFRICA TO THE AFRICANS

The people of Africa have not only been dispossessed of their history but they also have very limited ability to determine their future. But these peoples' creativity and energy, be it on a national or on a regional level, are certainly enough for them to reappropriate their destiny.

This battle will not be easy because Africa stirs up polarised positions where observers and African elites are driven to a binary logic and are called upon to choose between the camps of the Afro-optimists and the Afro-pessimists.

For some, often connected to the business world or to the diaspora, completely globalised and free to move as they please, Africa would be in constant movement and on the point of again taking charge of its destiny. They forget to mention that only a minuscule percentage (calculated by the World Bank to be barely 2%) of the population is involved in this dynamism and that the vast majority would have to content itself with living on the sidelines.

Others are experts, journalists and essayists, who are endlessly repeating that Africa is in bad shape, has got bogged down and, worse, is decaying. Indeed, the economic, social, educational and health context in many regions across Africa is disturbing. But, at the same time, the persistence of this fatalistic discourse feeds highly questionable prejudices about Africans - as people who would be condemned to decline by their very essence - that provide the framework for a thinly disguised racism.

And so the time has come to examine how we can find a more balanced discourse which is both nuanced and close to reality.

Who could be the Afro-realists?

They can't be found amongst the African intellectual media personalities in Europe and in the United States. These people, living in the comfort of their host countries and obsessed with their need for recognition, usually deliver non-controversial messages that often have been formatted for the exclusive use of Westerners.

These heralds of a disembodied 'global Africa' and promoters of racialist concepts of 'black identity' are far removed from the trivial realities of daily life experienced by the peoples in Africa.

If one wants to get a grasp of the complexities of African life, it seems to me that novels offer an invigorating pathway. The success of several authors writing in English, Portuguese or French who have won recognition in recent years by being awarded multiple literary prizes is but the visible part of a remarkable body of works by a large pool of African writers. Using works of fiction as a privileged way to access reality is a platitude, but regarding Africa it has become a necessity.

I can attest that works by Zimbabwean authors have prevented me from despairing when I felt the complete incomprehension which overcomes you when you live in Zimbabwe - they did this better than any analyses and any expert briefs.

Permit me now to recommend some of these writers: Tsitsi Dangarembga, Chenjerai Hove, Tendai Huchu, Doris Lessing, Yvonne Vera and others. Their novels have been my most valuable guides, giving me a way to escape from superficial preconceptions and reductionist anecdotes.

But there is more than these books. It is also encounters, most especially meeting Tendaï, that have allowed me to get a sense of the depth of pre-established ideas we have about Africa, be they from the continent or from abroad.

'We must unfetter our perception of ourselves to give our youth complete freedom to think. Our hopes are entirely in their hands.' This was Tendaï's constant refrain.

Despite all the economic difficulties, the political obstacles and the external constraints, Tendaï was sure that, while his generation had failed, subsequent generations would be able to learn all the lessons from his generation's failures. He argued for taking stock of all the post-independence African regimes, starting today, analysing without compromise the misguided ways of the recent past, and contesting all prejudices, be they of white, African elite or diasporic origins.

His contradictions - particularly his excessive respect for his hero Bob - did not prevent him from having a higher perspective and a capacity to challenge things commonly taken as self-evident.

He knew that public opinion, especially in Europe, had been established on the basis of pernicious approximations -Africa as an undifferentiated whole - which in effect denied the culture, history, existence, and soul of each African people. But he was not content with just harshly criticising the white world's toxic misunderstanding of the Africans.

Convinced that the soothing sleepiness was weakening the continent, Tendaï argued for the removal of all hulking ideologies, most especially Pan-Africanism and all colour-based claims that used black skin as the mark of identity.

To him, these ideologies prevent the only possible solution, which is for the peoples of Africa to take the necessary responsibilities in the framework of their respective nations.

During one lunch, he brought along a notebook full of passages from declarations by African intellectuals which he had found online in the course of his research. He hunted down any and all texts available online, as he could no longer obtain these books, which had become unavailable in Zimbabwe. Mockingly, he pointed at his notes.

'I'll spare you this passage where Africa is described as a geo-aesthetic entity... yes really... and this other one where Africa becomes global Africa in gestation, and this other one, look, which holds that the large cities in Africa will become world capitals. I've got a whole notebook where I recorded such definitive claims!'

He closed his notebook and continued.

'It's already so hard to know what it means to 'be African' that the quest to become 'Pan-African' has become an illusion. And what's more we are now transitioning to the stage of 'the global African'.'

He continued in a kind tone.

'Well, all that is not a big deal. They are dreamers, and

that's their right. But here they have no impact. They are selling their pitch in your society.'

I did not know what to reply. I had already observed the same thing in African cinema: filmmakers who were famous in Europe and made 'African' films for Europeans who celebrated them in all their festivals, but whose impact in their countries of origin had only been limited. As time went by, they were seen in Africa as European filmmakers, an uncomfortable situation which some of these filmmakers took very badly.

Tendaï took on a serious tone.

'And yet there is a little sentence that shocks me. It's from one of those African intellectuals who are adored in Europe.'

He searched his notepad and then found a page that he had scrawled on.

He read it aloud slowly.

"To a large extent the slave trade is indeed the event through which Africa entered modernity'. Don't you see the utter incongruity of that sentence?! Just imagine a Jewish intellectual writing 'To a large extent the Holocaust is the event through which Jews entered modernity'. It's inconceivable, isn't it? That person would be burned in the village square. With Africans, that's not even noticed. After all, this is just a black person talking about Africa. So it doesn't really matter.'

I knew that the passage in question was a quotation from Achille Mbembé, and I took to defending him, knowing how easy it is to take a quote out of context.

Tendaï shrugged his shoulders.

'Since he is so famous in the West, when you meet him one day, please tell him to stop talking about Africa as if it were one single country and about Africans as a single people.'

As much as Tendaï had convinced me that we should stop talking about Africa as an entity unto itself, I was to the same degree doubtful about the urgency of pushing aside Africanist thought.

Still, his words seemed true enough when I reflected on a pragmatic perspective for the future: 'first renationalise the history of each country in Africa and then make our collective future colour-blind'.

I would have loved to challenge Tendaï further on the question of collective African identity. But I really didn't have enough time to do this (see the following chapter).

REFORMING THE WAYS IN WHICH FRANCE AND THE EUROPEAN UNION ARE INVOLVED

My encounters with Tendaï and the vicissitudes of my daily life in Zimbabwe completely toppled all my certainties. Not only did I take a lesson in humility, but I also began to think differently about the presence of Europeans in Africa, a presence whose pertinence became ever less clear with each passing day, and especially my own presence.

It's not trivial to represent a former colonial power in Africa — and that was my job. It wasn't always an easy task, although I must admit that my stay in Zimbabwe was made easier by a declaration by Robert Mugabe in 2017 praising the sacrifice of French soldiers in their effort to fight Islamic terrorism in the Sahel. At the time, he was still president and I had just arrived.

It was easy to put up a good front to the world. On a personal level, it was a different story entirely. I never really felt I belonged there, a bit like an actor who is being paid to play an ambiguous role every day on the improvised stage of low-end theatre.

What startled me most was the conviction shared by every one my contacts, including my Western colleagues, that France was still a dominant power in Africa.

I tried to explain to Tendaï that France was in reality a declining power in Africa. These are supporting figures.

On the commercial level, France's portion of the commercial relationships between the African continent and the rest of the world declined from 10% in 2000 to less than 5% today. The number of French companies in Africa fell drastically and participation was limited to those who could afford to take known financial risks.

Taking a demographic look, there were several hundred thousand French expats in the 1980s, whilst today only 140,000 expats are registered with the French consulates. Even counting the non-registered individuals, I'm not sure we reach 200,000 French citizens present in these territories. Compare this figure to the 2,800,000 Indian, the 1,100,000 Chinese, and the 900,000 Portuguese people who are there. Even the Lebanese (500,000) outnumber the French.

To be sure, development aid is still a priority, especially to the French Development Agency, but this aid has been broadened to many other countries, which relegates Africa - and especially French-speaking Africa - to the status of one area amongst others.

And then there is 'your Macron', as Tendaï used to say, a bit condescendingly.

Certain events blurred the French president's message. There was his bearing during the exalted delivery of his speech in Ouagadougou on 28 November 2017, which was presented as foundational. There were his little maladroit comments on the fertility of African women, mentioned as a demonstration of a cultural problem. And then there was his questionable joke about the unfortunate Comorians who had risked their lives on makeshift boats to be part of the French island of Mayotte.

People in Harare paid close attention to all of this, even Tendaï.

I went to great lengths to point out that President Macron had good ideas about Africa - placing his bets on the young people, encouraging private businesses, striving for better support from the African diaspora in France. What my conversation partners remembered was the arrogance and the little wounding words.

Questioned on many occasions by Zimbabwe's late former minister of foreign affairs, S. B. Moyo, I dodged the subject by talking about the French president's youth, a foolproof argument on African soil.

So I tried convincing Tendaï of the slow but inexorable contraction of France in Africa. To no avail. He retorted, 'So why did you get involved in the Sahel?'

'Because neutralising Islamic terrorists in the Sahel means keeping them from destabilising western Africa and in this way the entire neighbouring area,' I replied.

Tendaï seemed only partially convinced. He took time to reflect before replying.

'Actually, for the Americans, you are in Africa what the

Kurds are in the Near East. You are their fighters in the field.'

Given the close military cooperation between France and the US in Africa, it was hard for me to explain to him how complicated this relationship is or was. And anyway, no matter what I would say, I knew that Tendaï would ultimately try to prove to me that it would be best for the French to pack up and leave.

Five years after our conversation, the chain of events in Niger, Mali and Burkina Faso would prove him right.

'Europeans should leave Africa' - that was always Tendaï's litany. And, based on the lively hatred of the former colonial power I sensed in Zimbabwe, I had no trouble imagining what the feelings toward France are in French-speaking Africa.

I do not want to cast doubt on President Macron's quick judgment, but the wounds of the colonial era remain alive even amongst the youngest. This situation largely explains why France is rejected. This rejection cannot just be chalked up to dishonourable Russian propaganda.

What should we do in the face of this receding tide?

Aside from the compelling necessity of setting a definite time limit for our military interventions - which our leaders have finally realised - it seems to me that we could pursue two main directions.

First, we need to fully accept our colonial past and stop minimising, denying and folklorising it or pretending that this past is behind us. Our historians, academics, politicians and, especially, the African diaspora that lives in France have a decisive role to play in this.

We also need to work to radically change the role of the EU

in Africa. France indeed has the political power and expertise to change the method of the EU's involvement so it no longer resembles that of an NGO. The EU could finally play the role one would expect of such a vast democratic area, and, what is more, one that presents itself as the largest trading power in the world.

The innovation would be that at last all the different development aids and financial supports from the EU and its 27 member states which were destined for an African country would be contingent upon the enforcement of the rule of law and guarantees of public liberties in these African countries.

This is not a question of exporting or imposing a democratic model - there are as many models as there are democracies - but of making the financial support hinge on clear juridical criteria regarding the rule of law and guarantees of public liberties which are made quantifiable and can thus be verified.

Driven by France, this would mean pushing the EU towards a Copernican revolution.

The sole aim of taking such a position would be to make it easier for Africans to take charge of their destiny in the face of autocratic regimes.

Some would say that the regimes in question would turn to Russia right away, but we must note that the Russians don't have sufficient means for their ambitions. The other alternative would be China, but China is getting a little more bogged down by African debt every day.

And we can't expect anything of the United Nations, dominated as it is by authoritarian states opposed to any changes in the status quo regarding the granting of financial support. In any case, UN agencies regularly call on their donors, most often the European ones. And so it's up to us to state our conditions.

As I see it, France's new path in Africa is rooted in the EU, an EU which strongly stands for its values.

When I mentioned these ideas to Tendaï, he reminded me that it took several centuries for the European governments to get over their urges for domination, for which they paid with many bloodbaths, first directed against their own population, then against other peoples, not to mention harming other continents.

'Why wouldn't the track record of African regimes be measured using the same yardstick that was used for that of their European counterparts?' he added.

I replied that today the African regimes don't have the long time that the Europeans enjoyed. They have to cope with constant pressure from the outside and especially with the impatience of their populations, which is increasing every day. The sudden intrusion of digitalisation in Africa makes this impatience all the more pressing.

FROM THE UNION OF AFRICA TO THE UNION OF ZIMBABWE

As I mentioned in the prologue, I was impressed by the resilience of the people of Zimbabwe, for whom shortages and suffering are their daily lot.

This resilience to misfortune remains a mystery to me. On many occasions I confessed to my conversation partners that I honestly didn't understand how the people of Zimbabwe could put up with such injustices. I never got a satisfactory reply. So I prefer not to present a superficial analysis of this phenomenon of submission/resilience, of which I evidently don't have a firm grasp.

But I did open up about this to Tendaï.

Before engaging in any reflection on this question, he established a non-negotiable premise. And he was right.

'The future of the people of Zimbabwe is entirely up to the people of Zimbabwe. No outside party should interfere to make decisions in our place, neither the Europeans, nor the Americans, nor the Chinese'.

So, I presented him with a simple hypothesis.

Zimbabweans living in Zimbabwe and in the diaspora are viscerally attached to their country. They are proud to be part of their culture and their history. They justifiably brag about the beauty of their lands, their flora and their fauna to the point of identifying with the bush, their mythical place of origin.

It's up to them to take action, with their demographic balance of power as an asset and their fight against corruption as a lever.

Their demographic handicap can become an advantage if the diaspora decides to play a more important role, beyond just sending money back home to their families.

The diaspora, estimated to be four to five million people, is spread mostly across South Africa, the United Kingdom, the United States and Australia. It is high in numbers and also high in qualifications. Zimbabwean expats are known to be competent and qualified and have a good reputation.

Moreover, in Zimbabwe itself, the people, be they lawyers, doctors, senior officials or just technicians, exhibit a degree of professionalism which impresses those who call on them.

The diaspora must finally become aware of its weight and then get organised.

To influence Zimbabwe and get things moving in the right direction, the diaspora has one great advantage: the ability to fight corruption. As long as that cancer continues to ravage the country's economy and social life, it would be an illusion to hope for any change.

But it's not all that difficult to mobilise specialised NGOs and well informed countries (such as the United States) to identify corrupt parties by name, trace all the networks of corruption and post this information on social media. That would definitely create an unwelcome climate for the corrupted and the corruptors.

Tendaï admitted that this would be a good thing but insisted that the political future of the country must involve the military and the Zanu. I agreed with him on this point. I did this for one reason alone: why add more suffering to the existing suffering by fanning antagonisms or by encouraging the equivalent of a civil war?

An open fight against corruption, both from inside and outside the country, is a great way to get some people to understand that Zimbabwe can no longer be treated like private property.

I think the time has come for a great national reconciliation in Zimbabwe: between the Ndebeles and the Shonas, between the diaspora and those living in the country, between the opposition and the Zanu, etc. But the prerequisite for this is to establish a new balance of power amongst the players, with the fight against corruption as its lever.

Instead of getting lost in the clouds of a hypothetical African union, working toward the unification of Zimbabwe seems to be a much more realistic goal.

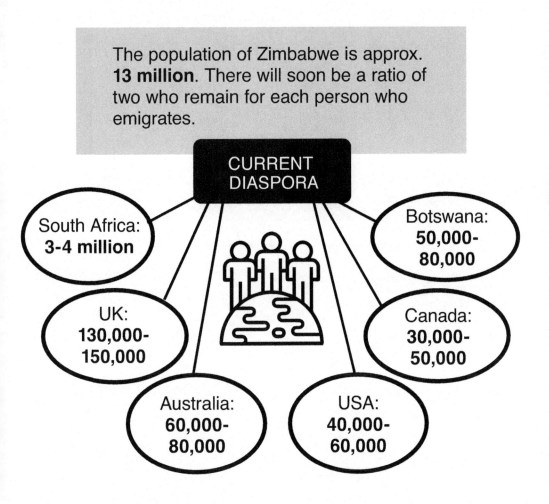

The population of Zimbabwe is approx. **13 million**. There will soon be a ratio of two who remain for each person who emigrates.

CURRENT DIASPORA

South Africa: **3-4 million**

Botswana: **50,000-80,000**

UK: **130,000-150,000**

Canada: **30,000-50,000**

Australia: **60,000-80,000**

USA: **40,000-60,000**

EPILOGUE

*'Black people aren't just
white people with black skin.'*
Yambo Ouologuem
Lettre à la France nègre
(Letter to the Blacks in France)

As I come to the end of this brief overview of the issues that preoccupied me during my brief stay in Zimbabwe, I must not hide a basic truth, and that is that I left the country filled with great frustration and a sense of failure. I must admit that when I left - full of regret - I knew only one thing for sure: this country did not need me at all, and I might have added, as Michel Leiris does in *L'Afrique fantôme (Phantom Africa)*, neither did the rest of Africa.

Yes, I can competently hold forth about the political and economic context of the country and trace back its recent history. But I know next to nothing of the deep identity of the Zimbabweans and what they really think.

Despite my attempts, I didn't manage to learn the Shona language. This means the scathing remark of Senegalese filmmaker Ousmane Sembene also applies to me: 'They occupied my country for decades and still don't speak our language; I'm the one who speaks theirs'.

I'm also not familiar with the foundations of their culture, their vision of themselves and of the world. I know little of their personal aspirations and even less of their relationship to their history and the history of other groups.

Even worse, despite all my attempts to create bonds with Zimbabweans beyond merely transactional ones (by increasing my everyday contacts with them), I never in fact crossed the threshold to what we might call friendship - not even with Tendaï.

It was as if there were an invisible, but impenetrable, glass wall, which I attributed to my position.

I learned to live with it. After all, that's how the world works. But this glass wall preoccupied me to the point that I mentioned it to Tendaï. His answer caught me off guard once again with a simple affirmation.

'Your status has nothing to do with it. You're white. That's all. That's the only way it can be here.'

To Tendaï, the glass wall was the result of white people's denial of black people's humanity; this denial showed up in the first interracial contact and was then theorised by thought criminals.

Kant, Voltaire, Hume, Hegel and Abbé Grégoire - this list unfortunately is not exhaustive - are amongst the European intellectuals who did not skimp on spreading sordid judgments about 'the Black African'. The same thing occurred amongst the philosophers of the Arab world, including the great Ibn Khaldun, whose degrading remarks about the 'black world' are on a par with those of their European counterparts.

But the authentic thought criminals emerged in Europe at the end of the 18th century and throughout the 19th century with the theoreticians of racialist doctrines.

The term 'thought criminals' is not mine. Tendaï, who must have memorised N.I. Painter's book on the history of white people, was very proud of it.

I had to face a self-evident fact: For almost three centuries Europeans had deliberately constructed an invisible apartheid between themselves and Africans where everyone was confined to their 'proper' place - even by force. Living next to each other was possible, perhaps, but never living together.

This glass wall was built deliberately, year by year, with the accumulation of all the suffering, humiliation, rape, and dispossession that men and women with black skin endured.

The British Zimbabwean writer Doris Lessing expresses this better than anyone in this quote from her book *The Grass Is Singing*: 'When it came to the point, one never had contact with natives, except in the master-servant relationship. One never knew them in their own lives, as human beings.'

What is the situation today?

I had an almost visceral feeling that this glass wall, deliberately theorised and constructed by Europeans, was still there, and solidly so, but that it had closed in on those who had invented it.

Of necessity, black people, rejected by white ostracism, ended up getting used to this invisible obstacle, finding in it a certain mental haven, a refuge from absurdity and arbitrariness. This segregationist partition boomeranged to turn against white people living in Africa. Crossing it has become more and more difficult.

There is now a paradoxical situation where, after black people, white people are now being marginalised in turn. Tearing down the glass wall will not be a small task, especially since it has evolved over many centuries.

I experienced this up close in Zimbabwe.

The first example of this is my relationship with Tendaï, who became my close conversation partner without ever becoming a close friend, no matter how hard I tried, taking any opportunity I could during our conversations to get closer to him and to his real life. He always dodged my attempts or changed the subject. This did not prevent us in any way from developing true intellectual closeness and honest cordiality for one another.

But this situation wasn't limited to Tendaï. I invited for lunch, dinner and breakfast countless Zimbabweans - ministers, high officials, members of parliament, lawyers, opinion leaders, entrepreneurs, farmers and others - down to people I met at the gym or at the market.

We talked, joked and exchanged ideas; we came to agreements and disagreements, talked about the future, always in a friendly and fairly direct tone; but things never went further.

In four years, only few returned my invitation and none of them invited me into their homes. When I was invited, it was always to a restaurant with this British quirk of starting dinner between 6:30 pm and 7 pm and always methodically ending the meal by 8:30 pm. This made it hard to create a closer bond.

Only the few mixed-race couples that I met were perhaps open to a less structured social relationship, but most of the time they were on the way out, wanting to leave Zimbabwe at any price.

I even tried to create a more personal relationship with the Zimbabweans who worked for the embassy. It didn't work. My status - but not only that - inhibited them.

Here is just one example: One day I called two Zimbabwean employees to my office, following two stupid mistakes they had made. Wanting to make an impression so they would not repeat the mistakes, I had asked an armed guard of the embassy to be there.

Hardly having entered the room, the two employees pushed themselves so closely against the back wall of the office as if they wanted to melt into it. They stood there with their heads lowered, shoulders drooping and faces full of fear. One of them, a strong man of about 1.90 metres, who could have slapped me to the ground with a single blow, called out twice in a contrite voice: 'Please, Sir, have mercy.'

I had the two of them sit down in two armchairs and tried to reassure them that there was absolutely nothing to fear beyond being scolded. I explained to them that, as local employees in an embassy, they had rights according to French law which no one - not even the ambassador - could touch. Even though this was the absolute truth, they didn't believe a word of it.

After a half-hour of soothing talk and a warm handshake from me, they left. When I was alone in my office again, I was the one who felt bad. My clumsiness had brought back a relationship of times gone by: being subjected to absolute white power. I was profoundly disgusted with myself.

So I investigated the situation. I talked to all my white Zimbabwean friends (of course they weren't 'Rhodies') - who had lived in the country for decades and who I knew had an anti-racist disposition similar to my own - and I asked them about this topic.

Most of them smiled at my naiveté. They gave me examples, whether from their professional or social lives, of daily relationships that were always courteous - the trademark of Zimbabwe - but never deepened beyond what was necessary for peaceful but distant cohabitation. They had made their peace with it. But I did not.

Back in Paris, I asked all the true lovers of African cultures I knew. All of them, without exception, had encountered this same problem.

Becoming friends - almost like family - where African friends open their doors wide and share their private lives with you is a rare thing. All of them said that they could count the number of their friends in sub-Saharan Africa on the fingers of one hand - if at all.

I am definitely not saying that this glass wall experience that I had in Zimbabwe is an iron rule that can be generalised to all of sub-Saharan Africa. Strictly speaking, I know nothing about that.

What I do know is how deeply frustrating it is to live in a country as fascinating as Zimbabwe and to live apart from its people.

I finally could open up to Tendaï about it.

In January 2020, I at last managed to convince Tendaï that a real restaurant would be a better place to celebrate the new year after all. He finally accepted my invitation to the restaurant Coimbra, whose Portuguese cuisine was appreciated by Zimbabweans of all classes.

I broached the topic of the complex relationships between black people and white people in Zimbabwe. Tendaï froze. I thought I had offended him with my clumsy approach - yet another discussion that started with the topic of skin colour!

But this was not the reason for his upset. The waiter had just brought a plate of grilled shrimp which horrified my guest and one of his nephews, who had come along.

'You aren't going to eat these horrid things, are you?' Tendaï uttered, with a gesture of disgust, whilst his nephew seemed frozen stiff.

I had forgotten that many Zimbabweans are disgusted by lobster, shrimp and other crustaceans in the way that Europeans are by grilled larvae, preserved spiders and snake meat. So I had the shrimp dish taken back to the kitchen. We returned to our perpetual grilled chicken with chips, which allowed us to peacefully continue our conversation.

He listened attentively as I opened up about this glass wall and its impact on everyone's daily life. I could even have talked about the relationship between the two of us if we had been alone, but the presence of his nephew did not encourage confessions.

This conversation remains burnt into my memory because Tendaï confirmed my intuition.

'What it takes is time, lots of time. You are right about the glass wall. It is a real thing. And it's not only between black people and white people. Even between us, Shonas and Ndebeles, there is a glass wall - not as thick and not the same as the one between you and us. But it's there as well. That wall will fall faster, of course. But it, too, will take time to happen. I think it must be the same throughout

Africa between the peoples who have experienced common painful histories. And it's the same between you in Europe. But it is true that between black and white people the barrier is higher and more consistent.'

I thanked him very much for his approach since nothing frustrated me more than simplistic debates where everything was reduced to skin colour.

He smiled and replied.

'I know just what you mean because I stand for making our collective future colour-blind. But at the same time we must be indulgent. Asking oneself how to be black in a fundamentally stifling white world is legitimate, isn't it?'

I confirmed. He continued.

'The difficulty lies in the expression 'to be black'. What does that mean? One doesn't say 'to be yellow'. You in France aren't asking yourselves if you are more or less white, are you?'

'We are and we aren't,' I answered. 'Fantasies of identity are also raging in France. People say a lot of stupid things about this topic.'

'I assure you, black intellectuals also say outrageous things about it, especially those in the diaspora. You should remind them of Fanon's words.'

He quoted from memory as follows:

'It's not the black world that determines my behaviour. My black skin is not the wrapping of specific values.'

I knew this Frantz Fanon quote from his book *Peau noire, masques blancs (Black Skin, White Masks)*. Tendai could also have quoted James Baldwin.

He broke out in hearty laughter.

'We'll discuss it next time. And you'll tell me what it's like for black people in France. But for now let's enjoy this delicious meal.'

I understood that he didn't want to pursue this topic in the presence of his nephew.

The three of us served ourselves another helping of grilled chicken and thick-cut chips.

Our next meeting, in February 2020, was very special. It was to be our last encounter, but I didn't know it yet.

He started out by telling me what the average person on the streets of Harare thought about the topic of skin colour.

'To the average Zimbabwean it's par for the course that black people are poorly treated in Western countries. Anti-black racism is simply experienced as the logical outcome of everything we've been through. Sad as it is, we cope with it as a matter of fate, just like droughts and floods. The paradox is that, in spite of this, there is still such a strong desire to emigrate. A lot of the candidates for emigration whom I know tell me that at least black people over there are free to protest, to make demands, even in the streets, whilst at the same time creating a future for themselves.'

He paused, waiting for my reaction. I did not react, however, not seeing what his point was. He continued.

'You see, that's my main criticism of those people who use only their skin colour as the basis to make demands. The injustices that black people face in Europe and the US are undeniable, and they occur in societies run by white people. But in Africa we have other types of injustice that are inflicted on black people by other black people. And defenders of the 'black cause' - he signalled air quotes - either forget to talk about this or do not emphasise it enough.'

'That's true,' I replied. 'Do you know the 'Global Blackness' movement in the United States that fights for solidarity and a type of common identity for all the people with black skin?'

Tendaï nodded in agreement and then replied, 'Yes, these people should be offered long-term traineeships in any country in sub-Saharan Africa.'

Tendaï went on in a weary tone.

'These people tire me out. When will they understand that reducing black people to the colour of their skin is a dead end? The name of the game is colour-blindness. Go ahead - tell me about what's going on amongst African intellectuals in France'.

After this outburst, I wasn't sure how I could present things to him.

I decided to take a higher perspective to get around my predicament.

'Black intellectuals in France are French above anything else. And, as such, they love pitting ideas against each other. There are many currents in the debate, but the two main ones at the moment are as follows. Some say the anti-discrimination movement must be universalist and based on the values of the republic. The others say that one must take into account in a specific way questions relating to physical features and skin colour. And, of course, there are extremists in both camps.'

Tendaï tried to pin me down.

'And you, what do you think of it?'

I hesitated with my answer, but, after all, it was a valid

question.

'I think we must bear in mind that France built its colonial empire in the name of universalist republican values. So we should be careful about believing in values that are presented as intrinsically virtuous. On the other hand, if your name is Mohammed or Fatoumata, discrimination and racism are a lot more real for you than if your name is Jean-Jacques or Agnès. But we must take care not to stick only to physical appearance and skin colour. Otherwise we risk locking ourselves into something called identitarian essentialism. In conclusion, I think these debates are very useful because they prove that French people of all colours and origins are constantly seeking to renew the social pact that binds together all of French society.'

'You're in luck. So, there's no glass wall in your country?'

'Of course we have one, but it's far from the one you have here. French society as a whole was built on the idea of integration, i.e. the slow but inexorable destruction of these walls.'

Tendaï seemed not to understand my explanation. So I tried to clarify my point:

'For some people the destruction of the wall, i.e. integration, is fast; for other people it takes more time. But the aim for both is the same: to become a French person, one amongst many. I can even tell you that I have friends of all skin colours and religions - and I've never felt a glass wall that compares to the one I am experiencing here.'

Tendaï remained puzzled for a long time.

'I'm not sure I understand, but I must admit that I've never really understood the white world.'

He paused and continued in a bitter tone:

'That doesn't stop white people from always wanting to solve our problems for us. As I've always said, you white people should stop interfering with our lives. As far as the glass wall is concerned, I think we should make it stronger.'

I didn't wanted to completely give up trying to understand him.

'The wall has prevented me from being integrated into your society, but it has not prevented me from getting a glimpse of the mental world of the people of Zimbabwe,' I replied.

He listened attentively as I spoke of the entanglement between the visible and invisible worlds that I first encountered when reading the novels of Zimbabwean writer Chenjerai Hove.

Shamanism is a powerful aspect of reality in Zimbabwe, as is the belief in prophecies and supernatural manifestations. I made the mistake of using the word 'superstitions'.

Tendaï interrupted me brusquely

'Be careful — you don't know much about this other reality since you Westerners have voluntarily cut yourselves off from the signals the world sends. So you call these 'superstitions' to protect yourselves from them. But you should know that there are invisible eyes and ears all around us. The world has its organs of perception. You mentioned to me many times the intense spiritual sensations you felt near Great Zimbabwe. This could be your point of contact into this parallel world. It's up to you to go there or not. In any case, I hope you understand why we are loath to excavate this sacred area, to turn it upside down, as you do with all things you do not understand.'

I took the opportunity to connect this with the topic of animism, which is described as the religion of 'the Africans'.

He replied, 'White people invented the word 'animism' because they believed that we celebrate nature out of fear of the spirits that inhabit it. They were wrong. This definition of animism is nonsensical. It only creates a category of religious inferiority, a catch-all to make us inferior to you. Nature has no particular spirit, human or not. There is only one thing, the world, which we are made of and which we make up. Without initiation, white people will never understand. They never will.' He repeated the last part for emphasis.

I did not like this smugness about esoteric knowledge. I replied animatedly, 'Animism or not, how do you explain the popularity of Protestant sects, Methodists, Salvationists, Evangelicals, Pentecostals and others, not to mention the crazy Apostolics?'

Indeed, a movement had taken off in Zimbabwe known as the Apostolic movement. The members of the movement wear long white robes, the clothes assumed to be worn by the first Christians, and meet at magical sites. They gather around a tree, a bush, or a rock and interpret the Bible under the guidance of a spiritual leader. This is a true sect with sexual rites and a blind allegiance to their self-proclaimed leaders. The Apostolic movement, which has been denounced by the Vatican, brings together hundreds of thousands of followers.

Tendaï took a moment to think before answering me.

'You're pointing at a flaw that charlatans like to take advantage of. They know that our bond with the invisible world guides everything we do, and they use this to take control of the weakest minds.'

He put an end to our conversation and repeated his previous interpretation.

'White people have banished the invisible world from their minds. Unless they get initiated, they will never understand.'

It reminded me of the question of where Christian faith comes from. The answer to that question is always the same: One must have experienced grace. Otherwise one just cannot understand. Be that as it may.

This relationship to the world seemed even more opaque to me when I learned that every Zimbabwean had a totem animal. It could be any animal: crocodile, lion, elephant, zebra, giraffe, etc. This was not a secret, and people talked about it very openly. But the consequences of this were incredibly far-reaching. Since everyone was convinced that their original ancestor was their totem animal, there followed lots of dietary restrictions, behaviour rules, particular bonds between totems and even rules for getting married.

In short, a person from Zimbabwe is at the centre of a complex system which ties together relationships between a totem, a clan, a tribe, the nuclear family and the distant family... a wide and interrelated world of relationships and family.

Come to think of it, reading the 1,700 pages of Livingstone's letters revealed to me another blurry area regarding the notion of tribe. What we call clan, tribe and ethnic group is in fact a shifting and subjective reality.

Livingstone writes about the notion of the tribe as being founded most often on a wide idea of kinship, which is real, but also often imaginary. It may also be structured around a vague common ancestor that may even be completely fictitious.

So he concluded that this notion of belonging is a lot more fluid and volatile than what we consider to be an inalterable bond. Livingstone had an intuitive sense about this throughout all his travels and describes the phenomenon admirably well.

As we did with animism, here, too, we have assigned definitive labels to spiritual lives and to social structures that we could not fully understand and, even less, recognise in all their complexity.

To us, these approximations have become unquestionable paradigms since we are so mired in our rationalist certainties.

Lastly, another question that fascinated me concerned the relationship with time. From what I have understood, the Shona language has two tenses, one for things that have been done and one for things that remain to be done (meaning there is no clear distinction between present and future). Although the languages are not related, it would be a bit as it is in the Arabic language, in which I used to be fluent.

I asked Tendaï, who explained it to me:

'It's true. The past is more important to us. It is the time of the ancestors and of tradition. We respect it. We tend to think of the future as a brief extension of the present moment. Living from one day to the next is one consequence of our rich vision of time. All you do is anticipate the future. But, as for the past, you care nothing about the past; it is 'passed', as you say - dead in a way. How do you expect us to come together?'

He broke out laughing.

This laughter will resonate in my head for a long time to come.

I wanted to go through this glass wall to understand what made us different. Maybe the most important and wisest thing to do is to just accept these cultural and spiritual differences as they are. I don't know anything about this. We are different from each other - and those differences cannot be reduced to skin colour alone - and that's a good thing.

After all, we must perhaps accept this glass wall.

I think that's what Tendaï wanted me to understand. Unfortunately I will never know.

In March 2020, Zimbabwe entered into lockdown due to the coronavirus epidemic. I waited for news from Tendaï for weeks. Nothing.

In May, the lockdown loosened its grip. I knew that Tendaï had contact with the waiter of a snack-bar that he frequented. The waiter informed me that his friend had returned to his village in a remote location in the northwest of the country, not far from the Zambezi river.

'Isn't there a way to get in touch with him through one of his nieces?'

The waiter replied in a mocking tone:

'The young people you met aren't relatives of Tendaï's. They are troubled youths that he was taking care of with his neighbourhood association.'

I was so taken aback that the waiter looked at me bemused, as if he were enjoying the trick Tendaï had played on me.

Desperate at the idea of never seeing Tendaï again, I gave money to the waiter in July and promised him much more if he could give me any news. Nothing.

That means Tendaï had either been killed by the epidemic, or the waiter hadn't been able to reach him, or, and this is what I feared most, Tendaï considered our relationship to be over.

At the end of August, before returning to France, I gave the waiter a long letter addressed to Tendaï. I also left the waiter my French mobile number so that I could be reached at any time.

I have not received any calls.
The wall has closed again.

THE END

RICHARD BOIDIN

Initially studying science, Richard Boidin enrolled in Oriental Languages at the Paris Institute of Political Studies (Sciences Po) and the Institute for Higher International Studies (Institut des Hautes Etudes Internationales) to qualify for the French Ministry of Foreign Affais (Concours d'Orient du Quai d'Orsay) in 1984 as a specialist in the Arab world and Africa. His first assignment was Baghdad, during the Iraq-Iran war, followed by a post at the Center for Analysis and Forecasting of the French Ministry of Foreign Affairs as an analyst for the southern shore of the Mediterranean.

In 1988, he became the international affairs advisor to Jack Lang at the French Ministry of Culture. In 1990, Daniel Toscan du Plantier, the president of Unifrance (an organisation promoting French cinema around the world), appointed him as his delegate general; and in 1994, Jérôme Clément, the president of Arte, appointed him as his director of cinema in charge of policies concerning purchases and co-productions.. In 2002, the French Ministry of Foreign Affairs appointed him to supervise all the foreign language programmes of RFI, TV5, CFI, the Fonds Sud and programmes intended for Africa.

In 2009, he became the representative for the information society and was responsible for defending French interests in international negotiations on digital issues. In 2013, he was appointed as the director of the diplomatic archives, where he initiated electronic archiving and increased the number of publications and exhibitions of the institution.

From 2016 to 2020, he served as the French ambassador to Zimbabwe and Malawi.

The author would like to thank Annouchka de Andrade and Marie Kuhn-Osius for their invaluable help in preparing this English publication.

MARIE KUHN-OSIUS

Marie Kuhn-Osius was born in New York, spent part of her childhood in Germany and is bilingual in English and German. She holds a Bachelor's degree in French from Beloit College and spent several semesters studying in France and Germany. She lives in France and has been working in the field of translation since 2006.